Company A Nineteenth Texas Infantry

A History of a Small Town Fighting Unit

David J. Williams, MS

HERITAGE BOOKS
2016

HERITAGE BOOKS
AN IMPRINT OF HERITAGE BOOKS, INC.

Books, CDs, and more—Worldwide

For our listing of thousands of titles see our website
at
www.HeritageBooks.com

Published 2016 by
HERITAGE BOOKS, INC.
Publishing Division
5810 Ruatan Street
Berwyn Heights, Md. 20740

Copyright © 2014 David J. Williams

International Standard Book Numbers
Paperbound: 978-0-7884-5698-5
Clothbound: 978-0-7884-6352-5

for Amanda

TABLE OF CONTENTS

LIST OF ILLUSTRATIONS

FOREWORD

When I was ten years old, my parents bought me a book, *The Civil War* by Fletcher Pratt, which was probably the first book I had ever read outside of school. After reading it, I decided that I wanted another book on the same subject. I ended up with *The Golden Book of the Civil War* from American Heritage. I was captivated. I began to seek out anything that was connected to the War Between the States. I discovered movies, such as *Shenandoah*, *The Horse Soldiers*, *Rio Lobo*, and the miniseries *North and South*. At a second hand store, I found a Dixie Gun Works catalog, a Tennessee-based company that capitalized on selling products related to the Civil War and early American history.

A few years later, I heard about people who dress in period clothing and recreate battles and I knew I had to find out more. In those days before the internet, a phonebook and a landline was the closest thing on earth to web searching. I eventually made contact with a nice lady at the Fort Worth Chamber of Commerce who led me to a local reenactor. At fourteen years old, I made my way into Civil War reenacting, first as a cannoneer in the Fifth Texas Artillery and then as a rifleman with the Southern Volunteers.

Although my life was briefly placed on hold while serving in the U.S. Army, I still made time to add to my historical collection and even take part in a few battle reenactments. That time, during the late 80s and early 90s, was the golden age for Civil War buffs. Some of the largest reenactments in history were held, new movies about the war were made, and Time-Life printed its classic Civil War series. I even began collecting the Franklin Mint's pricy Civil War chess set.

After serving in the military and starting a family, I had little time or money to devote to my passion. Luckily, I lived near Granbury, Texas, where I was able to participate in the city's annual Civil War reenactment. It was here where I made contact with the Nineteenth Texas Infantry, Company A reactivated. Captain Ricky Hunt, Corporal Ralph Falconer, and Private Joe Patman welcomed our family. Not only did I join the unit but I became enthralled with the history of the company that we portrayed.

When I decided to return to school, there was no doubt that I would study American history. In undergrad classes, I wrote papers on the Nineteenth Texas Infantry whenever possible. Later, in graduate school, I decided to make the history of the Nineteenth Texas Infantry my focus, which resulted in the work you are about to read.

My greatest hope is that reading this book might light a fire of passion in someone as those early books did for me so many years ago.

David J. Williams

ACKNOWLEDGEMENTS

Dr. Richard B. McCaslin, chair of the history department at the University of North Texas guided me through the process of writing this unit history. Whenever I was bogged down in primary sources or when I needed assistance in my search for additional sources McCaslin was there to point me in the right direction. Thank you, Dr. McCaslin.

Other professors who had an impact on my research, my style, and my ability to put my ideas on paper included: Dr. Gustav L. Seligmann, Dr. Alex Mendoza, Dr. Walter E. Roberts, and Dr. Randolph B. Campbell. Thank you, gentlemen, for helping me reach my goal of becoming an accomplished researcher and writer.

I would also like to thank my family for their encouragement and support while I studied. Thanks to my mom and dad and my children, Heather, Nathan, Carter, and Brooklyn, for the many days that they wanted to play or spend time with their dad that was studying, writing, or otherwise busy with an inordinate amount of research. Most importantly, my wife, Amanda, has encouraged me from the very beginning that I could do anything I set my mind to. Her faith in me, which is probably too great, helped keep me on the path toward the completion of this book. She endured many long days where she took full responsibility for three young children while her husband labored over a laptop with books spread about the room. Her support never wavered, and I will never forget her sacrifices she made for me.

Lastly, I would like to thank my Lord and Savior, Jesus Christ, for blessing me with the ability to complete this research and placing me in the midst of all the wonderful people who helped me along the way.

INTRODUCTION

The experience of Company A of the Nineteenth Texas Infantry, C.S.A., offers a unique opportunity to explore and, in many cases, debunk widely touted stereotypes of Confederate soldiers in the American Civil War, especially those from the Lone Star State. The majority of the recruits destined for Company A came from a real town, albeit a small one, in an otherwise overwhelmingly rural state. A study of these Texans provides a rare chance to explore a select group of men that do not fit neatly into the generally accepted typecasts and assumptions of general histories of southern soldiers. First, they do not fit all of the stereotypes concerning backgrounds and motivations that have been based on their counterparts from other parts of the Confederacy. Formed in a river port town, within the rural backdrop of East Texas, the company attracted recruits from an array of professions that more closely mirrored that of a small northern city than the agricultural society of the South. Second, their experiences do not always support the previous assumptions about such military topics as morale or the utility of repeated frontal assaults. Finally, their post-war careers offer a useful corrective to other studies, which abruptly end when the war concludes. In sum, this brief case study serves as a reminder that general studies do not always convey the whole story of service and sacrifice in the armies of the Confederacy.

While the motivation of the men of the southern states to join in the fight against what many called "northern aggression" has long been debated by many historians of the American Civil War, the argument of what motivated the average soldier serving in the Confederate military seems to have been resolved. Even though the centennial of the war in 1961 stirred these topics and brought a renewed interest to the study of the late war, a much earlier historian, Bell Irvin Wiley, laid the groundwork for those that followed in *The Life of Johnny Reb: The Common Soldier of the Confederacy* (1943). Not only did Wiley discuss the motivations of these recruits, but he also wrote about the "average" Confederate soldier in the Civil War. He analyzed data, letters, and other primary sources to provide the reader with a colorful narrative describing the typical soldier as a rural, farming, non-slaveholding, poor southerner.[1]

Just before the close of the 1950s, Shelby Foote, another highly respected historian and author of the volume series, *The Civil War: A Narrative*, continued the arguments found in Wiley's work, presenting the South as an underdeveloped region with cotton as king and farming the primary source of income. Foote's ideal southern soldier was an experienced outdoorsman, an able horseman, and handy with a gun. He additionally portrayed the North as an industrialized center populated by factory workers and rising entrepreneurs, eschewing agriculture for the progress of machines in the factory.[2]

Although fears of invasion and conscription have been the most cited reasons for a renewed movement for volunteering into Confederate service in early 1862, historians have long debated alternatives to the prevailing wisdom. This debate has resulted in its own historiography, which Charles David Grear traced in the introduction of *Why Texans Fought in the Civil War*. Wiley, one of the earliest authors to study this motivation, concluded that the southerner's resentment of the North's aggressive political policies and their desire for adventure were the dominant reasons for volunteering to fight, which of course increased from 1861 to 1862 as ill feelings toward the Union intensified in the South. Shelby Foote, while not mentioned in Grear's historiography, repeated Wiley's logic, and he even cited *The Life of Johnny Reb* in his introduction as an instrumental source for his classic narrative. Grear's chronology continued with James I. Robertson's *Soldiers in Blue and Gray*, which added state's rights, as well as regional or state pride, to the list of motives in addition to the already mentioned avoidance of conscription. James A. McPherson, in 1987, wrote what would become regarded as one of the most highly respected titles in the field of Civil War history, *Battle Cry of Freedom*, in which he shifted the direction of the argument by placing more of an emphasis on slavery as a motivating factor. Later historian's arguments included religion, honor, home, and hearth.[3]

While Wiley, and then Foote, undoubtedly pioneered in defining the Confederate soldier, many more historians would soon follow, either building on their foundations or, in some instances, arguing against those earlier assertions. McPherson, in his epic *Battle Cry of Freedom*, and subsequent works, including *For Cause and Comrade: Why Men Fought in the Civil War*, presented arguments regarding the causes of the war that tended to stray from those of Wiley, but his descriptions of the backgrounds of soldiers in both blue and gray followed the same pattern, contrasting those who came from northern urban centers of trade with men raised in southern rural agricultural communities grounded in a slave economy. Indeed, McPherson stated that less than one-tenth of the southern population lived in urban areas, towns by today's standards, while more than one-fourth of the citizens north of the Mason-Dixon Line lived and worked in industrialized cities.[4]

More recent, Texas-centered historians of the Civil War have attempted to highlight the uniqueness of their state, while also emphasizing its similarities with the remainder of the Confederate states. Ralph W. Wooster, not unlike Wiley, pioneered the study of Texas as a unique part of an overall very complex region. Wooster, in *Texas and Texans in the Civil War*, initiated a series of Civil War publications that describe the Texas experience during the war. While Wooster maintains that Texas' experience was similar on many levels with that of the other southern states, he also argues that Texas was unique in its position on the frontier, its international boundary, and its population of hardy pioneers, primarily from southern states. This idea of Texas, as the Lone Star State, helped fuel the contemporary notion that Texans were different, and as such, they should maintain that distinction in the ranks.[5]

Other historians have added countless publications focusing on Texas as a unique region within the larger framework of southern states. Richard G. Lowe and Richard B. McCaslin have been instrumental in bringing the Texas experience during the Civil War. Their works have brought the "unique" stories of John S. "Rip" Ford (the Texas Ranger turned Confederate colonel that fought Indians, Mexicans, and Yankees during the war) and Walker's Texas Division (the only division of the war comprised of only Texas men) to students and Civil War enthusiasts across the nation, which have undoubtedly added yet another layer to the Lone Star enigma of Texas as an exclusive region. Grear went even further and added the unique notion of "multiple local attachments," meaning that Texans, due to their recent immigration into the state, held more than one town or state as their "home."[6]

Building on this academic foundation laid in previous years, this work focuses on one of the most unique military units in Texas, and possibly the Confederacy. Company A of the Nineteenth Texas Infantry was one of the hardest fighting units of the Confederacy's Trans-Mississippi Department. The men that formed the regiment during the spring of 1862 joined other Texas regiments in Arkansas and later became the core of the famous Walker's Texas Division. Sharing the unique traits of Company A, the division was the only such unit in the Confederacy that was comprised exclusively of Texans. What set Company A apart from the rest of the Nineteenth Texas Infantry was its recruitment primarily of men from Jefferson, Texas. Jefferson, the seat of Marion County, was the largest inland city of the Lone Star State in 1860 and a bustling center of commerce. The urban dwellers that served in Company A were the most diverse part of the regiment, with merchants, lawyers, pharmacists, newspaper men, silversmiths, and entrepreneurs serving next to rural farmers from the county. Company A became a unit that defied the norms established by previous historians, creating a uniqueness that mirrored that of the Lone Star State.[7]

The first chapter of this study focuses on the creation of Company A and the Nineteenth Texas Infantry. Company A, along with the regiment, formed in the spring of 1862, which indicates that the members enlisted in partial reaction to the series of military setbacks experienced by the Confederacy in Kentucky, Arkansas, Louisiana, New Mexico, Tennessee, and along the massive coast of the southern states. These young men left their homes, their women, and their jobs in part to reverse the string of Union victories and secure southern independence. Also compelling these men to volunteer for this new regiment was the rumor of conscription, which soon proved to be true, and the threat of being forcibly assigned as replacements in previously formed units from

Texas. Whatever their individual reasons may have been, the regiment organized and trained just outside of Jefferson, where the companies drilled together before marching off to Arkansas.

The next two chapters discuss the military operations of Company A, in which these Texans, along with the remainder of the division, after a slow start in Arkansas, would be involved in multiple major engagements, including Perkin's Landing, Milliken's Bend, Fort DeRussy, Mansfield, Pleasant Hill, and Jenkins' Ferry. The original commander of the regiment, Col. Richard Waterhouse, would become a celebrated hero of the division, and be singled out by the brigade commander for his bravery and heroism, which resulted in his eventual promotion to brigadier general. Other men, both officer and enlisted, contributed to an impressive war record of hard fighting every time the regiment faced the enemy on the field, adding to their high reputation among Confederate troops. At the same time, their repeated success in frontal assaults, along with the light casualties suffered by Company A, undermines the bitter criticism of Civil War leadership that appears in works by McPherson and Russell F. Weigley, among others.[8]

But that is not where this story ends. The last chapter chronicles the experiences and contributions these men made after they surrendered their arms and shed their Confederate uniforms. Company A's service record within Walker's Texas Division, as impressive as it was, was perhaps not the most important legacy these men left behind. An astounding number of the veterans from Jefferson and its surrounding communities left a record of civil service and entrepreneurship second to none. Not only would the company contribute several attorneys, railroad magnates, and highly successful businessmen, but the unit also spawned Texas legislators, Democratic Party leaders, Electoral College members, and Gilded Age philanthropists that left behind charitable organizations that are still changing lives today.

Truly, the veterans of Company A who survived the war could stand proudly among their peers. But at the same time, they were not necessarily just like their counterparts from elsewhere in the Confederacy. Their experience challenges several stereotypes concerning Confederate soldiers, and their performance may in fact provide additional evidence to substantiate the high demand of Walker's Texas Division among the army leadership and their ability as Texans to drive the enemy from the field. Company A, in the Lone Star tradition, stands out as a true Texas anomaly.

CHAPTER 1

GENESIS OF A CONFEDERATE COMPANY

Texans volunteered for service in the Confederate armies in tremendous numbers. By the end of 1861, there were more than 25,000 men in Confederate uniforms from the Lone Star State. Most of these volunteers served in the cavalry because Texans tended to prefer mounted service. But there were important infantry units as well. For example, out of this initial rush to arms came the famous Hood's Texas Brigade, which would fight in Virginia, ultimately with Gen. Robert E. Lee's Army of Northern Virginia.[9]

Not only did Texas contribute an enormous fighting force, but the state also played a pivotal role in supplying food, weapons, and clothing to troops throughout the Confederacy. With the exception of New Orleans, the eastern ports of the Confederacy were the first to be targeted by the Union navy. With blockading forces threatening harbors from Virginia to Georgia, Galveston became a very popular port for ships avoiding the heavy guns of the

Union fleet. Nearly as popular was the overland trade route of goods that were shipped to Matamoros and taken across the border and through Texas in wagons and carts.[10] Military supplies from Europe were extensively traded in this manner, and this equipment was used in almost every theater of operation in the Confederacy. But, while supplies and trade routes were vital to the Confederate cause, men for military service became the most important contribution that Texas made to the rebel nation.

When Abraham Lincoln took the oath of office as president of the United States in March of 1861, the provisional government of the Confederacy had already been formed and its representatives were meeting in Montgomery, Alabama, debating the relations of their government with that of the United States.[11] Their decision to avoid a war with the United States was important due to the unprepared state of the Confederacy. Unfortunately for them, by April 1861, Lincoln's policy to "hold, occupy, and possess" government property, and his demands to "collect the duties and imposts" from ports across the southern states, had made war unavoidable.[12] When Confederate forces fired on the federal troops in Fort Sumter, both nations issued calls for volunteers to bolster their respective armies. The Confederate Congress authorized President Jefferson Davis to enlist existing state militias and create new state volunteer regiments to add to a small regular army already in service.[13]

With the election of Lincoln in 1860, the southern slave states' leaders had feared that further restrictions on slavery and other intrusions would hurt their economies, which led to the first wave of secession. Quickly following South Carolina's lead, Texas was the last of the first group of Deep South states to secede early in 1861. These were the seven states whose delegates met and formed the Confederate States of America in March 1861. Four more joined the original seven after the firing on Fort Sumter and the call for volunteers. With the formation of the Confederate States of America and Lincoln's determination to preserve the Union, the stage was set for the long and bloody American Civil War.[14]

As mentioned earlier, by the end of 1861, more than 25,000 Texans had joined Confederate service. While the exact numbers are disputed, approximately 90,000 Texans would eventually join Confederate cavalry, artillery, or infantry outfits, or enlist in state organizations. The first Texas units to join the Confederate cause were recruited by three celebrated Texas Rangers, Ben McCulloch, Henry E. McCulloch, and John S. "Rip" Ford. These three leaders were appointed as colonels by the Texas Committee of Public Safety. Among their first Texas volunteer commands were the First Regiment of Texas Mounted Rifles and the Second Regiment of Texas Mounted Rifles. While these commands earned distinction for becoming the first Texas regiments transferred to the Confederacy, these men were deployed to the unglamorous frontiers of west and south Texas. Other regiments were formed to march east to join the Confederate forces at Richmond and in the western theaters in Kentucky, Tennessee, and Arkansas. The First, Fourth, and Fifth Texas Infantries became the only Texans to fight in the eastern theater. Organized into a brigade, they soon earned fame as Hood's Texas Brigade in General Lee's Army of Northern Virginia. Texas troops that left their home state during the fall of 1861 also included regiments destined for Arkansas under the command of the legendary Ben McCulloch and the Army of Mississippi under the command of Albert Sydney Johnston, himself a Texas legend and the highest ranking field general in the Confederacy.[15]

The Texas troops, with their commanders, celebrated the Confederate victories on the battlefields of First Manassas and Wilson's Creek in the spring and summer of 1861. During the spring of 1862 the early successes of the Confederacy were suddenly offset by setbacks in New Mexico, Arkansas, and Tennessee, which represented an overwhelming defeat of the Confederate military. The losses included the deaths of the two popular Confederate generals who were legends in Texas, Albert Sydney Johnston and Ben McCulloch. After the battle of Pea Ridge, where McCulloch was killed, the Union command took control of northwestern Arkansas, and at Shiloh Maj. Gen. Ulysses S. Grant's army forced the retreat of Johnston's forces all the way into northern Mississippi. In New Orleans, the Union navy forced the surrender of the largest port city in the Confederacy. Invasion routes were opened into all areas of the trans-Mississippi region of the rebel nation, in which Texas lay. The Confederate victory at the First Battle of Manassas had now been eclipsed by Union troops marching into every corner of the Confederacy's western states.[16]

These defeats had a sobering impact on citizens in the South. New recruiting drives arose all over the region. In Texas, both infantry and cavalry regiments were raised in even larger numbers than in 1861. Patriotic rushes to arms came to a feverish pitch, with Texans alarmed that Union invasions into the state appeared inevitable as defeats on the battlefield opened the doors to eastern Texas and its coastline.[17] Perhaps the most radical reaction came in the form of conscription. The Confederate Congress passed the first conscription law in April 1862. Men that were conscripted were to be placed in previously formed units that had been depleted by casualties and desertions. Comparing the numbers of recruits to that of conscripts, it appears that most men preferred to fight with friends and family from the same city or county, so, volunteering for service in a newly formed company was clearly more popular than waiting for conscription officers.[18]

While not everyone in Texas enlisted for the same reasons, it would be reasonable to conclude that most of the spring 1862 enlistees into the Nineteenth Texas Volunteer Infantry Regiment (Nineteenth Texas Infantry) were motivated by a desire to avoid conscription and to protect their communities from Union invasions like those to the north and east. Richard Waterhouse, who would be elected colonel of the Nineteenth Texas Infantry, wrote his wife, Rose, often giving her frequent updates on the men and their mission. In one letter, written during the Red River Campaign, he said that he wished to expel the invader from southern soil and protect his family in Texas. Pvt. Joseph P.

Blessington, who would obtain fame writing the first account of the Texans' experience in Walker's Texas Division, argued that he "by force of arms" sought to "preserve untarnished the principle of constitutional liberty" and free Texas of "despotic domination of Radicalism."[19] Of the four officers in Company A, only two owned slaves, while all of the men were either upper middle class or wealthy by 1860 standards, with one officer in the highest economic bracket. This would indicate that while they may not have fought for slavery in 1861, they certainly had much to defend from any Union invasion in 1862.[20]

In 1977, Randolph B. Campbell and Richard G. Lowe, both distinguished professors of early American history, wrote a ground-breaking study of wealth and income distribution in Texas prior to the Civil War. This study becomes important by offering definitions of class structure in Texas. *Wealth and Power in Antebellum Texas* defined the poorest class as those who own less than $500 in property, the middle class as those falling between $500 and $19,999, and the wealthiest class in the state as those who had more than $20,000 in property and assets. These classifications will assist in analyzing the men that formed Company A in the spring of 1862.[21]

While the unique status of Company A's enlisted men will be discussed later, a brief description of their officers' backgrounds can provide a useful start. Capt. William L. Crawford, a non-slaveholding resident of Jefferson, was a successful merchant and recent graduate of McKenzie College. At the outbreak of the war, Crawford was studying law under David B. Culberson, a popular attorney in Jefferson who had served as a delegate to the secession convention in Austin. Crawford, with a family net worth of over $25,000, was one of the few men in Company A that fell in the wealthiest bracket defined by Campbell and Lowe (and he also appears to have been the only original captain in the Nineteenth Texas Infantry with a college degree). His brother, Meriwether Lewis Crawford, who also became instrumental in the formation and maintenance of Company A, was an educated, aspiring attorney in the spring of 1862. After the war, these two brothers would add to their illustrious careers by becoming prominent Dallas lawyers and politicians.

The Crawford brothers were not the only leaders of Company A with wealth and status. William J. Clark, who succeeded Crawford as the captain of Company A, had a home in Harrison County worth $3,000 and other personal property doubling that amount, including fourteen slaves. Working as a farmer in Marshall, he had built a substantial homestead and even employed a farmhand to help maintain the estate. First Lt. Joseph McDermott, a single man in the company, was a property owner, and quite wealthy in comparison to most of his mess mates. McDermott worked as a merchant and apparently had a substantial mercantile business in Jefferson worth more than Clark's farm, but he did not own slaves. Second Lt. Miranda W. Covey's property is not valued in the census but he is listed as owning thirteen slaves, which undoubtedly placed him in the upper middle-class. Covey's status in the community as a leader was already evidenced by his participation in the Democratic Party as a delegate to the National Convention that selected John C. Breckenridge as the presidential nominee from the southern wing of the party.[22]

The enlisted men that joined Company A of the Nineteenth Texas Infantry in the spring of 1862 did share one important quality with the earlier recruits of the fall of 1861: age. Of the recruits into Company A, thirty-five percent can be found in the 1860 census. Additionally, the age at enlistment of the recruits can be found on the majority of the service records of the men of the Nineteenth Texas Infantry, maintained by the National Archives. Of the available records, the roster of volunteers for Company A shows that eighty-eight percent of the men were equivalent in age to the previous summer's enlistments from 1861. Although recent scholarship, including Richard G. Lowe's *Walker's Texas Division*, argues that the recruits of 1862 were significantly older, more likely to be married, and more likely to be land owners than those that joined in the first year of the war, Company A's data does not validate all these allegations.[23]

According to Bell I. Wiley, a pioneer in the study of the lives of Civil War soldiers, the average age of the men who served in the Confederate armies was 26 years old.[24] The average age would include those young recruits in the first years as well as the old men who volunteered or were drafted in the closing years of the war. The average age of the recruits into Company A was 25.7 years old. This figure places the company's members close to Wiley's average, and again counters the generally accepted belief that the troops of 1861 were younger. The recruits of Company A ranged from a boy of 16 years old up to one gentleman who was 46 years old when he enlisted. This is a very wide range, and the high ages of a few men tends to pull the average age up. Actually a majority of the soldiers in Company A were in their early twenties when they signed the muster rolls in Jefferson, which is much younger than the average age as reported by Wiley.[25]

The youngest known recruit in the company was John B. Snow, who joined at the tender age of 16. Snow signed the muster roll on July 29, much later than the majority of enlistees who had enlisted in March 1862. Surviving records do not indicate the story behind this but because the military did not accept recruits under age 17, it is possible that Snow was a runaway, joining the company just days before they marched out of town. He did not give his age to the recruiters since he was so young, probably to ensure that he would not be turned away, but he is found in the United States Census in 1860. Young men in isolated communities were, in many cases, very susceptible to disease. The Texans marched to Rondo, a small community in Arkansas, in the late summer of 1862. By the spring of 1862, Union armies were campaigning simultaneously to capture Little Rock, Arkansas and Vicksburg, Mississippi, and the Nineteenth Texas became active in the attempt to thwart these invasions. Snow, the youthful private, was reported sick and left behind until he was able to make the journey to Little Rock. He finally recovered enough to reunite with his company near the Arkansas capital, but he lapsed back into his previous illness and died on February 28, 1863.[26]

The oldest recruit into Company A was Charles F. Renean, who enlisted as a private in the company on March 31, 1862. According to his service records, Renean, whose name appears to have multiple spellings, was frequently detailed for service that would not require the strength of a younger man. He worked as a nurse at the hospital in Jefferson for an undisclosed time before being sent to work with the supply train, likely as a driver. Late in the war he was working at the quartermaster depot back in Jefferson.[27]

A breakdown of the rest of the troops in Company A will also present evidence that contradicts the prevailing arguments concerning the ages of the 1862 recruits as well. As illustrated, there were very young members in the company and there were older or middle-aged men as well. There is also concrete data for seventy-five percent of the seventy-eight original members of Company A. This gives the researcher substantial information with which to analyze the age of the men in a variety of ranges. Almost thirty percent of the recruits were under 21 years old, and adding recruits as well who were under the average enlistment age of 26 creates a cohort of fifty-four percent of Company A. More important, just twenty-one percent of the recruits that enlisted were over the age of 30, which indicates that there really were very few older men in the company.[28]

As previously mentioned, the average age of recruits into the company was 25.7 years old, which again puts these enlistees just under the average age of Civil War soldiers. The largest single age group that enlisted into Company A was eighteen year olds.[29] This could be due to the habit of young recruits to lie about their age and claim the accepted age of eighteen so that recruiters would not reject them. The median age group for Company A included men that were between the ages of 26 and 35. Twenty-two men fell into this age range; therefore, 25 percent of the company would be slightly above average age for recruits but not necessarily middle-age or too old to perform their duties. This number, again, is equivalent to the percentage of the earlier Texas units that were raised in 1861.[30]

The final age group would be those who were over 35 years old when they enlisted. They are interesting because they would not have been subject to the conscription laws in the spring of 1862. There were ten of these men, and they accounted for eleven percent of the company. This is substantially lower than that of Company H of the 1st Texas Infantry which enlisted in the fall 1861.[31] The fact that the men in this age range would enlist early is consistent with a popular theme of 1861. Most politicians and newspapers indicated that the war would last only three months, in turn, those who were getting older would have likely signed on earlier in the conflict if they wished to take part before the war was over. Again, the motivation for these 1862 recruits is uncertain, but it appears that the largest number of Company A's recruits were very young and therefore would fit into Wiley's arguments that they were seeking adventure rather than defending their property.[32]

While Company A mirrored other Confederate units in the age category, regardless of when they were recruited, that seems to be where the similarities end. The troops from Jefferson maintained their unique identity regarding their profession, property ownership, and marital status. With the aforementioned limited census data, fourteen men can be positively identified as married, reflecting more than forty-five percent of the company. Again, this number is much higher than the figures of earlier recruits as analyzed by Wiley and Lowe.[33] Regarding land or real estate ownership, ninety percent of the married men and thirteen percent of the single men owned personal property, with more than 83 percent of those identified qualifying as middle or upper class, which an extremely high number for a Confederate company in the Trans-Mississippi.[34]

Although only thirty-five percent of the seventy-eight recruits in Company A are found in the 1860 census, a systematic analysis of this sample will provide some insight into the men that enlisted in the spring of 1862. The bulk of Company A was recruited from Marion County, Texas. Six men can be traced to Upshur County, two lived in San Augustine County, and one each came from Buchanan County, La Grange County, Liberty County, and Milam County. One man, due to a friendship in Texas, crossed over the state line from Caddo Parrish, Louisiana, and joined the company. Jefferson, the seat of Marion County, was a bustling commercial town, which apparently led to a large percentage men from Company A working in careers other than farming.

The professions of Company A's recruits is a key distinction that sets the company apart from the rest of the regiment. While some men were not identified in their occupation in the 1860 census rolls, those that were identified included eight farmers, three merchants, four clerks, three laborers, one carriage maker, one mechanic, one silversmith, two carpenters, one printer, and one druggist.[35] The available records indicate that while there were, of course, farmers in the company but they only made up less than one-third of the officers and men, a notably small percentage in an era when market agriculture was king, especially in the South. Almost 70 percent of Company A's recruits maintained professions as varied as shopkeepers, merchants, clerks, laborers, carriage makers, mechanics, silversmiths, carpenters, printers, and druggists, many of which would surpass their farming counterparts in their ability to earn substantial incomes, some as slave owning farmers.[36]

The breakdown of Company A's officers has already been divulged, but in summary, eight men were elected to commissioned officer status from Company A. Of these, three men's wealth is unknown, with two of those unknown likely to be very secure financially, with one being a well-respected citizen of Jefferson, Texas. The other two cannot be determined with available data. With the remaining 63 percent, one man is in the highest class with more than $24,000 in property, with the other four being well established in the upper middle class.[37]

Company A was also composed of several enlisted men with property and wealth. More than 75 percent of the non-commissioned officers and enlisted men held status as middle class citizens, leaving a very small number of men in the lowest economic bracket. Sgt. Silas H. Nance was an accomplished farmer owning almost $3000 in property in 1860. Pvt. A. L. Hopkins entered service with over $3,500 in assets. Pvt. N. S. Morgan entered service as a man of moderate means with $600 in assets, placing him in the middle class. Pvt. William Peters, an up and coming local merchant, held a moderate business with $800 in property. Ennis Ward Taylor, who entered the company as a private and was quickly elected lieutenant colonel, held substantial wealth as a druggist with $8,000 worth of property.[38]

Perhaps because of their backgrounds, Taylor was not the only member of Company A who later assumed greater responsibility within the regiment and brigade. William L. Crawford, the older brother of Meriwether L. Crawford, enlisted in the spring of 1862 and was quickly elected company commander. His dedication to service led to his promotion to lieutenant colonel, and he commanded the regiment by the end of the war. G.T. Mott, who lived with his friend and fellow recruit, Aaron Smith, at the beginning of the war, served faithfully in the company until he was detached to work in the Jefferson Quartermaster Depot in April of 1865. Smith, who was working as a store clerk, was quickly identified after his enlistment for his bookkeeping and inventory skills and appointed captain and quartermaster for the regiment before

14

he ultimately fulfilled those duties for the entire brigade, which put him in a very powerful position. Many others were often detached as teamsters, clerks, and other skilled positions. All in all, the company was composed of many talented, dedicated soldiers, many of which would leave a legacy of service even beyond their original assignments.[39]

Company A certainly appeared, in many ways, to be an unusual unit within the Confederate army from its inception, but the organization of the Nineteenth Texas Infantry, which mustered in May of 1862, overall exemplified the recruitment drives across the South after the series of setbacks in the western and Trans-Mississippi Theater. Joining many other Texas infantry regiments, including the Tenth, Eleventh, Twelfth, Fourteenth, Sixteenth, Seventeenth, Eighteenth, and the Twenty-Second, the men of the Nineteenth Texas formed the Texas Division at Austin, Arkansas in October 1862. The Texas Division was further divided into three brigades; the First Brigade under the command of Col. Overton S. Young, the Second Brigade under the command of Col. Horace Randal, and the Third Brigade under the initial command of Col. George M. Flournoy and later the command of Brig. Gen. Henry E. McCulloch. The latter was the home of the Nineteenth Texas Infantry (brigade command would evolve during the war with promotions, demotions, and transfers within command structure).[40]

Company A did share a unique attribute with the other troops within the division, which became the sole division in the Civil War that was comprised of only Texas men. The unit became known as "Walker's Texas Division" after Maj. Gen. John G.

15

Walker was placed in command in January of 1863. Because of their speed on the march, these fast-marching Texans also became known as "Walker's Greyhounds" and the "Greyhound Division."[41] The division served only in the Trans-Mississippi region of the Confederacy, where it was also the first Confederate unit that faced black troops in combat.[42]

Most of the companies of the Nineteenth Texas Infantry shared the rural qualities of the typical Texas regiments formed in the spring of 1862, while Company A maintained its distinction as a fighting force that contained more small town professionals. The regiment enlisted ten companies from East Texas; each company was given a letter designation from "A" to "K" with no "J" company due to military tradition. The first company to be formed, Company A, was very different than the rest of the regiment. Although a few of the men in Company A came from rural counties, including Anderson, La Grange, Milam, Robertson (which provided the highest percentage of farmers in the company), Rusk, San Augustine, Titus, and Upshur, the majority of the Company A's recruits lived in or near Jefferson, Texas, in Marion County.[43]

Jefferson became the center of much of the recruitment activity for Company A, and later the organization of the Nineteenth Texas Infantry, because of its size and location. In 1862, it was a prosperous river port community located on Big Cypress Bayou. The town had grown considerably in the years leading up to the Civil War and had been selected as the county seat of newly created Marion County in 1860. What is unique is that Jefferson, roughly 200 miles from the Gulf of Mexico, became a major inland port that conducted a tremendous amount of trade with New Orleans and Shreveport, Louisiana, via the Red River and the Big Cypress Bayou network that flowed right into downtown Jefferson. A prewar rush of commerce caused Jefferson's population to explode as men of all professions made this East Texas town their home.[44]

Busy Jefferson served as a proper stage for the formation of one of the most celebrated regiments in Walker's Greyhound Division. The Nineteenth Texas Infantry was mustered into service in May 1862. The men quickly elected Richard Waterhouse to be the colonel of the regiment on May 13, 1862.[45] Waterhouse was a prominent citizen from San Augustine and had worked with his father in the mercantile business before the war.[46] In addition to his family business, Waterhouse had served as teenage runaway in the Mexican-American War and as a Texas Ranger with the famous Col. John S. "Rip" Ford on the Rio Grande. His family had become well known in the area and his father would be elected to the Texas Senate the following year. Waterhouse, likely with aspirations for higher rank, had enlisted in Company C of the Nineteenth Texas Infantry at Jefferson on March 31, 1862, which appears rather unusual due to his acquaintance's and friend's enlistments into Company A. Waterhouse's prominent associates in Company A included Crawford, Clark, McDermott, and Covey, among others. As colonel, Waterhouse's influence over his junior officers, and former business associates, was great, even leading to Clark's transition into the mercantile business after the war.[47]

The men trained in a large open field near Jefferson, which was christened as Camp Waterhouse in honor of their newly elected colonel. While some companies of the regiment were assigned various details taking them away from active duty, Company A served with the regiment for the duration of the war. Upon its enlistment, recruits were assigned to their company streets at Camp Waterhouse, where they began intensive training in the manual of arms and other military basics. While the duties were exhausting, knowing that their families were nearby and made frequent visits to the camps was comforting to the men.[48]

Many of the men, especially the farmers, had limited exposure to diseases due to their relative isolation in east Texas. When mustering into service, they were exposed to many contagious diseases for the first time, leaving thirteen members of Company A dead by late 1862 and several others suffering. The suffering began while in the training camps around Jefferson and intensified when the Texans marched into Arkansas in response to various threats from several converging Union forces that were attempting to occupy Little Rock. Pvt. Meriwether L. Crawford of Company A, the twenty-one year old brother of the original company commander, became sick with dropsy.[49] His condition was so bad that when the company marched for Arkansas during the late summer of 1862 he was left at his home in Jefferson to recuperate. Colonel Waterhouse, as regimental commander, detailed Crawford as a recruiter in Jefferson until he was able to return to his company in May 1863. Crawford must have been a capable young man due to the fact that even with his sickness he worked tirelessly in a variety of positions. After returning to active duty with the regiment he was again noted for his exceptional qualities. During the Battle of Pleasant Hill, he was badly wounded and was cited for heroism. His actions were recognized by then General Waterhouse, who had been promoted to command the Third Brigade after the death of Brig. Gen. William R. Scurry at the Battle of Jenkins' Ferry. Crawford also received a promotion to serve as the general's personal aide-de-camp in October 1864. He performed these duties until the following spring, when he signed his parole and left for his home in Jefferson.[50]

The problem of illness became ever more acute after the Nineteenth Texas reached Arkansas. Prominent recruit Miranda W. Covey, who was elected as the second lieutenant for Company A, became sick on the march to Arkansas and was left behind at Pine Bluff in early 1863, when the regiment moved to its new winter quarters. He was lucky enough to recover from his undefined illness, and he rejoined his command just in time for the spring campaign season. His duties for the company included requisitioning supplies through the quartermaster department in his home town of Jefferson, from which Crawford regularly corresponded with him. Covey served with Company A until he was wounded late in the war, when he was sent home to recuperate while the company was camped at Hempstead, Texas, during the last months of the conflict.[51] There are no records indicating where he was wounded but it is likely

19

that he was one of the many casualties at Jenkins' Ferry, where the regiment suffered its highest losses.[52]

Among those who fell ill when Company A marched to Arkansas were two very homesick brothers. Pvt. Marshall N. Dale enlisted with his younger brother, Jefferson E. Dale, from Titus County when the company was formed. Both men had joined the Texas State Militia as part of the Eighth Brigade in July 1861. Apparently wanting to be members of an actively campaigning infantry regiment and seeking adventure, the young men headed for Jefferson the following spring. Arriving at Camp Waterhouse, the men settled into their new life in the military, which was very different than serving in a state militia company in which a soldier would typically only drill part-time and march only when called upon by the governor. Now the Dale brothers drilled endlessly, performed work details, and took breaks solely at the pleasure of their company commander. This new lifestyle did not sit well the new recruits and shortly after their arrival in Arkansas both men were listed as sick. Later their unhappiness would lead to more tragic results for both of them.[53]

In the final analysis, the recruits that enlisted in to Company A during the spring of 1862 brought an element of uniqueness to the Nineteenth Texas Infantry, primarily through its members' diverse professions and high percentage of wealthy men. These atypical recruits of Company A would eventually march off to war, where many of them would succumb to disease and a few would struggle with their loyalty to "the Cause." All of them suffered from loneliness and yearned for the end of war, while those that survived would feel the sting of defeat and return home to rebuild their lives.

STEAMER C. W. BENTELL, OWNED AND OPERATED BY B. W. MARSTON. PICTURE IN CYPRESS BAYOU ABOUT 1881. JEFFERSON, TEXAS.

Jefferson, Texas, in the late nineteenth century (Courtesy of Marion County Chamber of Commerce)

William Lynne Crawford, Captain, Company
A, 19th Texas Infantry, and his brother,
Meriwether Lewis Crawford, Private,
Company A, 19th Texas Infantry
(Courtesy of Texas A & M University
Commerce)

CHAPTER 2

"My Loss is Truly Deplorable and My Very Heart Sickens at This Contemplation"

The Texans who joined Company A of the Nineteenth Texas Infantry during the spring of 1862 were well aware of the dangers they would soon face in Confederate service. Jefferson, the center of their recruitment activity, was also the home to multiple newspapers, which printed accounts that highlighted the death and destruction on the distant battlefields of Virginia and Tennessee. Indeed, the Battle of Shiloh, the bloodiest battle to that point in the war, was fought and became headlines in the local newspapers while these businessmen and farmers were filing into recruiting stations in town. While the Confederate government frantically attempted to fill the ranks of the army with conscription, these Texas volunteers were rushed into training camps outside of town. They were then sent to Arkansas within a few months of their enlistment. Without much more training, Company A, along with the rest of the Texas troops, endured their first battles at Perkin's Landing and Milliken's Bend during the late spring of 1863.

After less than three months of formal training and with no shortage of community celebrations for the new recruits, the regiment was ordered into action. Before leaving Jefferson, politicians and local leaders organized festive banquets where the men were fed, patriotic speeches were delivered, and regimental colors were presented by fetching young women from the community.[54] During August 1862, after the festivities subsided, the men marched to Arkansas, where they were ordered into more training camps near Austin, north of Little Rock. As the Nineteenth Texas Infantry made its way to Camp Nelson the soldiers were greeted by locals who encouraged them and sometimes provided food for the hungry troops. Where they drilled and were later assigned to the Texas Division, initially under the command of Brig. Gen. Henry E. McCulloch.[55] Before their first fight, Maj. Gen. John G. Walker, fresh from the Army of Northern Virginia, was placed in command of the huge green division, while McCulloch was reassigned to lead the Third Brigade, which included the Nineteenth Texas. Not only would Walker's name soon become synonymous with the division, but his leadership would help create one of the most effective fighting units in the Trans-Mississippi.[56]

Before the regiment arrived in Arkansas, Confederate forces in the northern part of the state were attempting to thwart a Union invasion force commanded by Brig. Gen. James G. Blunt. Blunt and his Army of the Frontier. Intent on capturing the state capital, Blunt defeated Maj. Gen. Thomas C. Hindman's Confederate forces at Prairie Grove in December 1862 and forced a general retreat toward Little Rock. While northwest Arkansas was thus secured by Federal forces, Confederate outposts on the Mississippi River were also being threatened by additional Union armies from above and below. When Company A arrived in Arkansas, and was attached to Walker's Texas Division, it quickly became engulfed in a confused and desperate military situation. Confederate leadership in the Trans-Mississippi Department was woefully inadequate and there was little agreement as to the primary threat that the Texans would have the greatest strategic importance. This indecision influenced the first orders to the division in December 1862, which instructed the Texans to march to the relief of Vicksburg, the Confederacy's last major port on the Mississippi River.[57]

The Texans marched and countermarched, receiving conflicting orders that kept the entire division out of every battle for the vital river bastion that the Confederate leadership had hoped to influence. The men's morale sank as they became ineffective puppets in the confused hands of Maj. Gen. Theophilus H. Holmes, head of the Trans-Mississippi Department. After being ordered back toward Little Rock, thus missing the chance to reinforce the garrison at Vicksburg, and arriving near Arkansas Post just after the surrender of the Confederate forces there, the weary regiment settled into winter quarters at Pine Bluff.[58] There they remained for the remainder of the winter of 1863. During this time, President Jefferson Davis replaced

Holmes with the more popular Lt. Gen. Edmund Kirby Smith.[59] After Union threats developed above and below the Texans' positions, Smith ordered the Greyhounds to a new position in Monroe, Louisiana, where they would be able to react quickly to any threatening force of Federals.[60]

The winter of 1863 was an extremely painful experience for the Texans. The Nineteenth Texas lost nearly 20 percent of the regiment in fatalities due to disease alone, while Company A lost another twelve men, or just over 15 percent. Among those recuperating from sickness were Jefferson E. and Marshall N. Dale. When they became well enough to travel, the Dale brothers packed and left for Texas. The division was losing a significant number of troops to desertion in 1863, and orders came down the chain of command to hold courts martial to try the men caught leaving their duty stations. Both Jefferson and Marshall were caught and tried in February 1863. They were sentenced to die by firing squad, which had become an all too familiar sight in the winter of 1863.[61] President Jefferson Davis pardoned the older brother, Marshall, but only after he saw his younger brother executed before his eyes. The pardon issued to Marshall was not uncommon after there were execution orders issued. During the American Civil War, approximately thirteen hundred death sentence convictions were approved by the Confederate courts martial; of those Davis pardoned more than six hundred. Those executions that were carried out served as harsh reminders of the dire consequences of desertion, and therefore encouraged the other troops to remain true to their units. But Marshall was stubborn. On September 6,

1863, he deserted from the company camp at Bayou Cotile in Louisiana and made his way back to Titus County, where he remained in hiding for the duration of the war.[62]

While Walker's Texans adjusted to military life in spring 1863, Maj. Gen. Ulysses S. Grant's Army of the Tennessee intensified its efforts to capture the Mississippi River region and isolate the western Confederate states of Texas, Arkansas, and Louisiana. Grant had spent much of the previous year attempting to march down to Vicksburg from Memphis, but his efforts were stymied by swarming Confederate cavalry under Maj. Gen Earl Van Dorn. Subsequent Federal efforts to bypass the bastion on the Mississippi, Vicksburg, by rerouting the river and digging canals were also unsuccessful.[63] By the spring, however, Grant had changed his tactics and established a new supply base at Milliken's Bend, located just a few miles northwest of Vicksburg. This time Grant would cross the Mississippi River, march east, and then face the smaller Confederate army on open ground in Mississippi, outside of the fortress city. Confederate authorities were concerned, and public pressure from many of its citizens demanded action.[64]

Attempting to emulate the success of Van Dorn's raids on Grant's supply line, General Edmund Kirby Smith, as commander of the vast Trans-Mississippi Department, ordered Walker's Texas Division to march toward Vicksburg and destroy Grant's supply line at Milliken's Bend on the west bank of the Mississippi.[65] General Walker, a veteran of the Mexican War, had been recently promoted and reassigned to the region. He already

27

had achieved fame during the Sharpsburg campaign under the command of Gen. Robert E. Lee when he had led his two brigades into Miller's notorious cornfield. His actions that day secured him a promotion to major general and a transfer to the distant Trans-Mississippi Department, where he took charge of the division that would immortalize his name. His arrival led to the reassignment of McCulloch, who resumed his command of the Third Brigade, to which the Nineteenth Texas was assigned, because he was less experienced and ranked lower than Walker.[66]

The new division commander led his men into what would be their first combat operation in the late spring of 1863. With marching orders in hand, Walker began making preparations for conducting his operations against what was thought to be the critical depots supplying Grant's army on the move now again against Vicksburg.[67] Indeed the supply line had been linked to the western shore, but before the Texans even started their march toward eastern Louisiana, Grant had rerouted his supply lines to come down the Yazoo River some fifty miles east of the Mississippi. So, before the Texas troops even began their campaign, their potential for success had already slipped away from them.[68]

Brig. Gen. Henry E. McCulloch
Photo courtesy of Richard B. McCaslin

On May 28, 1863, Walker's Texas Division (three brigades then commanded by colonels Overton S. Young , Horace Randal, and George M. Flournoy) began boarding transport vessels that moved the Texas troops through Louisiana by way of the Little River, Black River, and finally Tensas River to within twenty miles of the besieged port city of Vicksburg. The operation was simple: using their cavalry as scouts, the Texans were to locate and destroy any Federal camps on the west side of the Mississippi.[69]

On the morning of May 31, Brig. Gen. Henry E. McCulloch, recently placed in command of Colonel Flournoy's brigade, roused his men from their sleep and led them on a forced march in the direction of the river, whence reports had come in that the Federals were in heavy force at Perkin's Landing about twenty miles south of Vicksburg. Upon arriving at that place, the Texans formed a line of battle and began advancing on the Yankee camp. Pvt. Joseph Blessington later wrote, "The enemy seemed not to anticipate our coming until a few minutes previous to our arrival, as they left precipitately, leaving behind them their provisions and cooking utensils. Our troops helped themselves to the enemy's hardtack and coffee." The Confederate advance went through what minutes before had been a relaxed Federal camp. McCulloch, however, soon noticed that there was an ironclad, the *Carondelet*, providing cover fire for the Federals, who were awaiting a transport vessel to carry them to safety.[70]

Cautiously, McCulloch ordered his artillery, under the command of Capt. William Edgar, forward with infantry support from Col. Richard Waterhouse's Nineteenth Texas Infantry. Waterhouse's men were anxious to get into the fight, and they cheered as the battery unlimbered. The artillery, which consisted of only two small six-pounders, began lobbing shells into the retreating Federals as well as the *Carondelet*. Col. Richard Owen, in command of the Sixtieth Indiana Infantry and approximately 300 contraband slaves, had only minutes to prepare a defense against the Confederate assault. His men stacked cotton bales on the levee so they would have some cover from which to fight the Confederates until transports arrived. Luckily for Owen and his men, just after the shelling began, the *Forrest Queen* arrived and began withdrawing the beleaguered Federals.[71]

Col. Richard Waterhouse
Photo courtesy of Richard B. McCaslin

When McCulloch learned that the Federal troops had escaped aboard the transport, he ordered his artillery to stand down and sent his infantry to plunder the camp, destroying what the men could not carry. McCulloch sustained losses of one killed,

31

two wounded, and two missing, with Colonel Owen's losses being eleven killed and about the same number of wounded. [72] This had been the first real action most of the Texans had ever seen, and both the Nineteenth Texas and Company A had suffered no losses. At the same time, they had earned high praise from their new brigade commander for their valor in standing fast as the assigned defender of Edgar's guns. McCulloch wrote in his official report that "They did their duty nobly. . . [the] men stood up under fire like a wall of masonry." However, their real test was just around the corner.[73]

After destroying the Federal camp, McCulloch moved back to his base camp on the Tensas River. The Texans immediately began preparing for their next offensive in the direction of Vicksburg. Maj. Gen. Richard Taylor, who commanded the Department of Louisiana, had come to the region to take personal command of the expeditions against the Federal encampments on the west bank of the Mississippi River. He was given inaccurate information by his scouts, which prompted him to divided his relatively small force and send the three Texas brigades in different directions to attack positions at Young's Point, Lake Providence, and Milliken's Bend. The reports given to Taylor led him to believe that the enemy positions along the Mississippi were garrisoned with fewer soldiers than were actually there. Also, the brigades were given poor directions to the sites, hampering their movements thereby losing the element of surprise.[74]

Fortunately for the Texans, their opponents were not in much better shape for a fight.

Stationed at Milliken's Bend was a Federal detachment under the temporary command of Col. Hermann Lieb. Just a few weeks before the Battle of Milliken's Bend, Grant had created the Department of Northeast Louisiana and placed Brig. Gen. Jeremiah C. Sullivan in command. One of Sullivan's most arduous tasks was enlisting and maintaining control of ex-slaves from the region. Milliken's Bend was in the center of this complex situation. The Federal camp contained many black slaves who had been forcibly recruited from nearby plantations. The black soldiers, many of whom were accompanied by their spouses, had been constantly threatened with violence from the white Federal troops encamped with them. After multiple cases of assaults against the men and their wives, including several sexual assaults, Col. Isaac Shepard of the Tenth Illinois Cavalry had one of the white soldiers whipped in the camp. The outrage of a white soldier being beaten by blacks was too much for his superiors to bear, and Sullivan ordered Shepard's arrest and called a court of inquiry. Although Shepard would later be cleared of any wrongdoing, he would become a sideline participant in the upcoming battle, his regiment's only action of the war.[75]

While enduring the plague of command instability, the Union troops stationed at Milliken's Bend had to remain vigilant against Confederate attacks. The depot had earlier been very important to the Federals during their campaign for Vicksburg, but by the time the Confederate high command had decided to attack, the small garrison had become almost insignificant in

Grant's operations. Lieb's disgruntled force was composed of the Ninth and Eleventh Louisiana Infantry (U.S.C.T.), two companies from the Tenth Illinois Cavalry and the Twenty-Third Iowa Infantry, for a total of 1,061 effectives.[76] The Union troops had the advantage of a strong position, using the river levee as breastworks with cotton bales stacked on top, reinforcing the already formidable positions. Complementing the defenses were two Union gunboats, the *Lexington* and the *Choctaw*, just down the Mississippi River with powerful guns that could throw 100-pound shells into any attacking force. [77]

Advancing upon the Federals was McCulloch's Third Brigade, which included the Sixteenth, Seventeenth, and Nineteenth Texas infantry regiments and the Sixteenth Texas Dismounted Cavalry, in all about 1,500 men. These men had been in the service for over a year and had marched hundreds of miles, all the while being deprived of deployment into any substantial action. Only the Nineteenth Texas had been close enough to the fight at Perkin's Landing to call themselves veterans. The adrenaline was running high as these Texans prepared to go into action.[78]

The two companies of the Tenth Illinois cavalry left Milliken's Bend late on the 6th of June, 1863, in search of rebels rumored to be in the area. McCulloch encountered these two companies at 2:30 a.m. on June 7 and quickly brushed them aside. Falling back toward their base camp, the Federal cavalry met Colonel Lieb with his Ninth Louisiana (U.S.C.T.), which had marched out past Walnut Bayou. Lieb feared being overrun in his

34

position and he had decided that yet another reconnaissance in force was his best option. However, when he discovered McCulloch's entire brigade, he began to rethink his actions. Lieb's men and the cavalry were in a precarious situation, as they were in danger of being cut off from the rest of the garrison. He immediately had his men form a battle line behind a thick hedge, which he used to conceal his position.[79]

When McCulloch's skirmishers arrived, after chasing the cavalry for some 500 yards, they were rudely greeted with a powerful volley from Lieb's concealed regiment, causing the Confederates to retire to their main line, which was already advancing toward the hedge. Colonel Lieb had temporarily turned the tables on his opponents, but the full force of Texas infantry had not yet arrived. The recruits of the Ninth Louisiana watched as McCulloch's men moved toward the ditch at right-shoulder-shift in perfect, parade-worthy formations. The coolness of the advance and the precision drill of the Texans bearing down upon them proved chilling to the green Federal troops. Many of the Union troops could not bear the sight, and they began breaking for the rear.[80]

Lieb attempted to calm his force and use the advantages that the ground afforded him. Marching out that morning, he had noted that there was a series of ditches and canals with nearly impassable, thorny bois d'arc hedges that he could use as natural defensive works to slow any attacking rebel force. At each of these positions, as he fell back, Lieb had his men take cover and fire a volley before retreating to the next ditch. The beautiful formations of McCulloch's brigade were soon disrupted due to the heavy fire and almost impenetrable hedges they encountered. Lieb, not wanting to be cut off from his path to the river landing via the Walnut Bayou Bridge, which he had crossed earlier, did not let the advancing Confederates get too close before each withdrawal. McCulloch's men gained confidence as they apparently forced the bluecoats from each of their positions one-by-one, taking light casualties in the advance. When the retreating Federals had made it about half way back to their camp, scrambling cavalry detached from the Tenth Illinois came running pell-mell for the rear, being chased by advance Confederate cavalry.[81] Lieb ordered his men to fire a volley and push the pursuing Confederates back toward their lines. Shepard then watched helplessly as his former command was routed from their positions. After the near disaster, Lieb withdrew his troops again into new positions behind the levee, just a stone's throw from the riverbank.[82]

McCulloch, sensing a quick victory and only a hundred yards away from the Union lines, halted his Texans and prepared them for a final frontal assault. Many of the Federals, especially the Ninth and Eleventh Louisiana (U.S.C.T.), also known as the African Brigade, had only been in service a few days and up to this point had never seen action. Unknown to them, many of the Texans in the ranks facing them were experiencing similar emotions, but with such a long wait for a fight most of the latter were ready to do their duty.[83]

McCulloch ordered his men to fix bayonets. Cheers ran down the line as the general rode along the line shouting "Bravo, Bravo!" to the troops.[84] The order to charge came and the Third Brigade took the form of a confused mob due to the treacherous hedges crowned with thorns that caused the Confederates to temporarily stall in front of the Union positions, where they were staggered by a heavy volley from the defenders. Private Blessington remembered, "gaps are opened in the ranks, but they close again and move still onward; thus fighting from hedge to hedge, and ditch to ditch, to the main levee, where the enemy took position." [85]   Most of the Texans reached the enemy's works before the African Brigade could discharge a second volley, but then for a short time the Confederates found themselves pinned down at the foot of the levee. There was no getting through the mess of tangled razor wire-like briars that formed the perfect natural defenses. It seemed that the attackers might have to run for cover, but the Nineteenth Texas, on the far left of the line, discovered that directly in their front the Federal garrison had cleared a large opening for reconnaissance. This clearing became Lieb's worst nightmare as he watched the Texans take full advantage of the breach and pour into his works.[86]

The fighting along levee was some of the fiercest in the war.   Colonel Waterhouse's Nineteenth Texas was the first over the levee and as they entered "the most terrible hand to hand conflict."[87] Waterhouse, sword and pistol in hand, mounted the levee and shouted to his boys to get over the hill. The green regiments of black troops stiffly resisted the Texan onslaught for a short time, but soon the defenders realized that they were being flanked and began to fall back toward the riverbank.[88]   McCulloch's troops followed closely. Many of the Union troops were stabbed to death or shot down where they stood. One witness to the carnage on the levee stated that the battle was "fought mainly hand-to-hand. After it was over, many men were found with bayonet stabs, and others with their skulls broken open by butts of muskets."[89]   The Union defense of the levee collapsed, and the rest of the stubborn bluecoats began to break and run for the riverbank. Some of the Texans chased them to the shore, while others used the levee as protection and fired on their trapped foes. While scores of Federals were taken prisoner before they could reach the water, many ran into the water and were shot as they attempted to swim to the safety of the eastern shore,.[90]

About that time, two gunboats, the *Choctaw* and the *Lexington*, under the direction of Adm. David D. Porter, began sending 100-pound shells into the advancing Confederates. Solid shot, grape shot, and explosive rounds began to rain upon the levee that the Texans had been using as cover while they fired at the scattered remnants of Union defenders. The shells crashing among the nearly victorious Rebels were just too much to bear. They had nearly "gobbled up the whole party" of Federals when the feared gunboats began to literally rain on their parade.[91]   Realizing that complete victory was impossible due to the timely arrival of the gunboats, McCulloch decided to withdraw his men away from the far reaching shots coming from the river.[92]

Dead and wounded littered the landscape around the landing. The medical corps of McCulloch's Brigade, which took to the field at the commencement of the engagement, quickly retrieved many wounded and dying Texans, while the rest of the brigade sought shelter out of the range of the gunboats. Although the Texans did not achieve a complete victory, they had badly mauled the defending garrison.[93]

The battle tested the newly recruited black regiments. Many of the prejudiced northerners had thought the blacks would not fight. Those doubters were proven wrong. While many of the freedmen were "badly scattered," most of them had stayed and fought courageously. Brig. Gen. Elias S. Dennis, who soon replaced Sullivan as the commander of the Northeast District of Louisiana, said, in his official report "it is impossible for men to show greater gallantry than the Negro troops in this fight."[94]

The Confederate after action report was written by General McCulloch in which he highly praised the Nineteenth Texas for their part in the battle:

> In this charge Colonel Waterhouse with his regiment distinguished themselves particularly, not only by a gallant and desperate charge over the levee, but they drove the enemy, leaving the camp

covered with the dead to the very bank of the river...to the end of the engagement, the colonel behaved in the most gallant manner, and his officers and men seemed to catch the enthusiasm of their commander, and did their duty nobly; and gallantly upon every portion of the field.[95]

After the battle, the issue of the black soldiers' treatment by the southern soldiers became highly politicized. Reports by Union officers and rumors after the engagement claimed that the Confederate soldiers advanced against the black troops with cries of "no quarter." General Dennis said in his report that the Texans "were ordered to charge with cries of 'no quarter.'"[96] Charles A. Dana, Special Commissioner to the War Department, reported immediately after the battle that blacks were massacred on the field, which led to a rally of the black troops.[97] The next day, after consulting with Dennis, he retreated from his previous statement, writing that he was not sure if reports of Confederates murdering their prisoners were true or not.[98]

These allegations in fact were unsupported and appear to be politically motivated, as evidenced in part by the fact that neither Dennis nor Dana were present during the battle.[99] Additionally, official reports from the Union officers present at the engagement omit any mention of a massacre of black soldiers. The only reports of indiscriminate killings came from disgruntled soldiers from both sides of the engagement, and this was only after the report of General Dennis became known. Colonel Lieb and Colonel Shepard never reported any massacre or murder of black troops.[100] It should be noted that if there was any suspicion that the rules of warfare were violated then the commanding officers of the black soldiers would be bound to report such an atrocity, and likely would have done so with zeal due to the inability of the Union troops to maintain their defensive positions against an equally matched attacking force. Historians still struggle with this question; however, most argue that there was no massacre or execution of white or black troops after the battle. Primary sources written by those who fought there on both sides indicate that the action was violent and bloody, but there is no conclusive evidence proving that Confederate soldiers were racially motivated to murder surrendering troops.[101]

Most arguments claiming a massacre rely heavily on Dana's report of Confederate soldiers killing wounded black troops, while ignoring his about face on the issue the next day in a follow-up report. Dana's political appointment, an attempt by Lincoln to provide some oversight over generals in the field that were deemed suspicious, resulted in reports that are often exaggerated or completely false. For example, in another report on the action at Milliken's Bend, Dana claims that "General McCulloch died on the field from the effects of a wound." Brig. Gen. McCulloch actually survived the battle unscathed. With such misinformation, Dana's credibility in reporting facts must be impeached.[102]

Another report claimed that black soldiers were bayoneted by retreating Confederate troops at Milliken's Bend. Again, this claim was not supported by federal officers on the field. Dana, in his report, stated that the action was fought primarily hand-to-hand, which was primarily fought with the bayonet, which led to a high percentage of bayonet wounds that should not be unnecessarily connected to brutality by the Texans. One veteran, Lt. Col. Cyrus Sears of the Eleventh Louisiana Infantry (U.S.C.T.), claimed in his memoirs forty-five years after the battle that the Confederate soldiers carried a skull and cross bones flag into battle, signifying no quarter. There was no collaboration from either Lieb nor Shepherd supporting this strange allegation, making the assertion highly improbable.[103]

Casualty figures also cast serious questions into the alleged war crimes. Killed and wounded from the white regiments engaged at Milliken's Bend very closely approximate the numbers from the black regiments. Additionally, if there were widespread murders of injured soldiers on the battlefield, then the 250 soldiers listed in the after action reports as wounded would not have been there. The black troops that were captured were not treated as prisoners-of-war, however, and were returned to their owners from whom they had escaped in the weeks previous to the engagement.[104]

While the after action reports are great sources to gain details about the battle, both commanders made erroneous statements in their highly exaggerated reports. McCulloch claimed that he had fought between 3,000 and 4,500 Union troops. He also said that there were three gunboats shelling his men when there were actually only two on the scene (the other vessel was a transport). Additionally, McCulloch stated that he had inflicted over a thousand casualties in the defending force when that number equaled the total number of men engaged.[105] The Union reports were even less accurate. General Dennis reported the Confederate strength at 2,500, and claimed that General McCulloch and Col. Robert T. P. Allen, of the Seventeenth Texas, were both killed in the battle. None of this was correct. No matter what either side claimed, the end result was the same. McCulloch retreated, and the Union garrison was saved from complete destruction.[106]

In the end, McCulloch did lose 185 men in killed and wounded, or roughly twelve percent of his entire force, which is relatively low by Civil War standards for a frontal assault against a fortified position. The Nineteenth Texas sustained a loss of nineteen men, with two killed, eleven wounded, and six missing, or roughly two percent of the regiment. Company suffered one missing in action, R. N. Neal, and three wounded, Sgt. A. Bradshaw, Pvt. C. C. Malone, and Pvt. William Rollins. Bradshaw was eventually discharged from the service due to his wounds and sickness. Malone was wounded and reported by his officers as killed in action. Malone, however, survived his wound and was captured by the returning Federal garrison. After a lengthy stay in the Union hospital near Milliken's Bend, Malone was transported aboard a hospital steamer to St. Louis, where he died at Lawson General Hospital on November 2, 1863, due to his wounds and complications with disease. Rollins wound healed, and he returned to his company and surrendered with his command in April 1865. Neal never returned to camp and was never reported as a prisoner of war. Company A's officers eventually changed his status to "assumed" killed in action, though his remains were never recovered.[107]

On the other hand, Union Colonel Lieb lost 652 men in killed, wounded, and missing, which represented an astounding sixty-two percent of the entire force stationed at Millken's Bend. With these losses, it would not be unfair to say that Lieb's garrison was rendered ineffective and virtually annihilated. Union forces, however, with much greater resources in manpower, quickly reinforced the small post after the battle, and many of those who were listed as missing in action slowly filtered back into camp in the days following the battle, reducing the catastrophic effect implied by the initial casualty reports.[108]

Retreating from the field, McCulloch and his men marched back to Richmond, Louisiana, where they had camped the night before marching to their first big battle. The Texans marching back to camp were very different from the ones who left the same place early the same day. These men had been touched by one of the fiercest small engagements of the war. They had used their bayonets with skill and wielded the butts of their muskets as clubs. Behind the long columns of bloodied veterans were numerous ambulances carrying the dead and wounded from the horrible battle. For many of McCulloch's men, their first battle had been their last.[109]

Less than one month after the battle, Vicksburg, the Gibraltar of the Confederacy, fell to the United States. Defending the last bastion on the Mississippi River was no longer a strategic goal of the Confederate government. Henceforth, the Confederates would have to be satisfied in harassing river traffic and making the voyage down the Mississippi as hazardous as possible for Federals. McCulloch's Texans would find themselves performing those duties later that year.[110] As for the landing at Milliken's Bend, it would remain in Union hands for the remainder of the war.

The Battle of Milliken's Bend stands in history as the earliest incident of black troops in combat. The men of the relatively unknown African Brigade, in their struggle on the Mississippi, preceded the legendary black regiment, the Fifty-Fourth Regiment of Massachusetts Volunteer Infantry, in their campaigns in South Carolina. Although they would soon be eclipsed by other black units, they were celebrated in an engraving of the battle on the front page of *Harper's Weekly*.[111] Black regiments, with renewed support from northern politicians, would flourish after the engagement and eventually help turn the tide of war in the coming years.

Although the men of the Nineteenth Texas Infantry had no idea that this battle would change history and ultimately lead to the Confederacy's loss of the war, those Texans were undeniably changed due to their experience as well. The inexperienced recruits had known nothing but sore feet and boredom before they marched into the fight on the levy that hot June day. With Milliken's Bend a memory for the Texas Division, they would soon embark on their most impressive campaign of the war when they faced Maj. Gen. Nathaniel P. Banks's Army of the Gulf in the Red River Campaign.[112]

Although there is some renewed interest in the battle, Milliken's Bend remains a virtually unknown engagement except to those who closely examine the campaigns of the trans-Mississippi theater.[113] The actual battlefield has been eliminated from the map by the might of the Mississippi River. A lonely historical marker at Grant's Canal in Louisiana marks the engagement for those who venture into the sparsely populated region on the west bank of the river. The erosion of the battlefield adds to the already apparent mystery surrounding the events that unfolded on that fateful in June 1863.[114]

Assessing the battle is difficult because both sides lost so much in the small but intense engagement. Even though the battle took place near the middle of the war, most of the participants had never seen action before. Some of the black troops had only been in uniform for days, while the Texans had been marching across the region for more than a year without seeing real combat. With Union forces losing more than half their forces, the battle takes its place among the per-capita bloodiest engagements of the war.[115] Perhaps no other epitaph to the battle is more fitting than the words of General McCulloch when, after he had surveyed the damage done by the battle, he wrote, "My loss is truly deplorable, and my very heart sickens at this contemplation."[116]

"The Battle of Milliken's Bend," July 4, 1863, *Harper's Weekly*

Maj. Gen. John G. Walker
Photo source: deadconfederates.com
http://deadconfederates.com/2010/06/16/general-walkers-pardon/

CHAPTER 3

"If the Enemy Would Come Here We Might Make it Very Disastrous for Them"

Company A, alongside its sister companies of the Nineteenth Texas Infantry, faced its most difficult campaign of the war in the spring of 1864 after enduring months of low morale and harsh conditions. Assigned to Major General John G. Walker's Texas Division, known as the Greyhound Division, the regiment marched hundreds of miles, fought in three pitched battles and suffered ninety-one casualties, or roughly twenty percent of the regiment in a four-week period (miraculously Company A suffered no fatalities during this campaign). The Texans fought two different Union invasions, both Federal forces attempting to converge on Shreveport, Louisiana, the capital of the Confederate Department of the Trans-Mississippi, and defeated each army in succession, securing the region for the Confederacy for the duration of the war.[117]

50

From the regiment's mustering into service in the spring of 1862 through the early spring of 1864, the Nineteenth Texas Infantry had marched and counter-marched across Arkansas and Louisiana, missing virtually every opportunity to face the enemy in combat. Frustrated with the inactivity, Col. Richard Waterhouse wrote "If the enemy would come here we might make it very disastrous for them."[118] With the confused leadership of the Trans-Mississippi Department, regional Confederate authorities could not reach a consensus on the Vicksburg situation. Although unaware that the opportunity had already passed, Lt. Gen. Edmund Kirby Smith ordered the Texans to make their way to east Louisiana, where they would attack what was previously Maj. Gen. Ulysses S. Grant's supply lines.[119]

After seeing the Federal troops route at the skirmish at Perkin's Landing on May 31, 1863, the Nineteenth Texas was eagerly waiting for their opportunity to see action. The men did not have to wait long. On June 7, 1863, the regiment had fought its first major battle at Milliken's Bend, a former supply depot for the Grant's Army of the Mississippi. Here the Texans fought a desperate hand-to-hand engagement with Federal troops entrenched behind earthworks reinforced with cotton bales. After driving the enemy to the river and inflicting high casualties on the Federal defenders, Confederate troops had been forced to withdraw by gunboats. Perhaps because the regiment suffered relatively light casualties at Milliken's Bend, morale was high and the men were eager to test their merit again. Unfortunately for those high spirited soldiers, their

51

morale would soon sag as the realities of homesickness settled in and defeats across the Confederacy became known. It was almost one year before they would face the enemy again, and then the losses to the Texans were not so slight. [120]

After the action at Milliken's Bend, the Texans returned to Richmond, the town they passed through before the Mississippi River campaign. After a brief reprieve at Monroe, the Nineteenth Texas began a scorched earth campaign. The regiment destroyed property that might in any way have been of benefit to Grant's army at Vicksburg. After the regiment had finished its depressing work along the river in July, Maj. Gen. Richard Taylor ordered the concentration of all his available forces at Alexandria. The division was again moved by river transports to the town. While the Texans were on the march, Brig. Gen Henry E. McCulloch was transferred to Texas, where he would take command of the Northern Sub-district. Col. George M. Flournoy, of the Sixteenth Texas Infantry, again assumed temporary command of the Third Brigade while leadership decided on a permanent replacement. Finally arriving at their destination, the Nineteenth Texas bivouacked twenty-five miles to the southwest at Camp Texas.[121]

After a rest period of a couple of months, orders came down the chain-of-command that moved the division near Simmesport, Louisiana. While there, two more very important changes in command took place. First, on the company level, in October 1863, Capt. William L. Crawford was promoted to major, resulting in Lt. William J. Clark's elevation to captain, replacing the first company commander.

More importantly, the Third Brigade was assigned a permanent commander that temporarily lifted the spirits of the men. Brig. Gen. William Read Scurry was transferred to Walker's Texas Division and assumed command of the Third Brigade. Scurry replaced Colonel Flournoy, who had been placed in temporary command when McCulloch was transferred to a command in Texas. Like McCulloch, Scurry was a veteran of the Mexican War, but he was more distinguished than his predecessor as a Texas politician, having served in the Congress of the Republic of Texas and as a state legislator. More important, he had won distinction during the Confederate invasion of New Mexico and in the recapture of Galveston from the Federals. A Texas officer in Walker's Division, in a letter to his wife reporting Scurry's appointment to command the Third Brigade, commented, "He is a fighter and those who follow him will go to the Cannon's mouth."[122]

At this time, Walker's Texas Division was posted between the Mississippi and the Red River to harass river traffic. During the month of November 1863, the regiment was camped on the riverbank of the Mississippi. With a battery of field artillery and a division of infantry, General Walker faithfully performed his assigned duties. All riverboat traffic was considered enemy movements and, therefore, a prime target for the Texans. Many pilots and passengers were killed attempting to pass the gauntlet that the Confederates had formed. Some riverboat captains refused to travel the waters where the division camped. Union Gunboats attempted to dislodge the men, but the levee provided the needed protection from the exploding shells. The division's performance was stellar, and the Texans struck fear into the hearts of sailors that month.[123]

While the performance of the Texans earned praise from brigade and divisional staff, the long months of idleness took a toll on the division. Disease and desertion plagued them throughout 1863. Records indicate that twenty-seven soldiers, or roughly 35 percent, of the men from Company A reported sick during the long cruel year, many of which were ill in the early months of 1863 and were again on sick call in the fall of the same year. Most of the men recovered and made their way back to their posts, but four men succumbed to fevers and other ailments and were buried in Arkansas, and one more died when the Texans moved into Louisiana. Desertion was another epidemic the company faced. Boredom reigned during the last half of the year, and many soldiers simply walked away and headed home, especially after the men witnessed the horrible effects of widespread disease. Twelve men left their assigned posts, with less than half of those captured and tried in courts martial. Only one man, the previously mentioned Jefferson E. Dale, was executed, while the others, including his brother Marshall N. Dale, were reprimanded and placed back on active duty.[124]

With the end of the winter, the Nineteenth Texas was preparing, along with rest of the army in Louisiana, to fight Maj. Gen. Nathaniel P. Banks and his invading army from New Orleans. Banks was under orders to secure Shreveport, Louisiana, and East Texas for the Union and thereby liberate southern cotton to be sent to idle mills in New England. General Taylor, the commander of the Confederate forces in Louisiana, wanted to slow the Federal army until he could gather all of his forces in the area and make a stand against the potentially overwhelming numbers commanded by Banks.[125]

Banks advanced up the Red River with a combined army and navy force of more than 30,000 men. Taylor had about 9,000 troops. In an attempt to impede the Federals as much as possible, Taylor had a small fort constructed near Marksville on the banks of the river.[126] This hastily built yet incomplete defensive position, Fort DeRussy, was manned by men selected from throughout Walker's Division, including almost all of Company H of the Nineteenth Texas Infantry. Every regiment was forced to choose a given number of men from their ranks to delay the enemy. Acting as a rear guard, the men knew that those selected might have to be sacrificed to give Taylor the time he needed to plan his next move. While the balance of the division marched north to relative safety, 350 men at Fort DeRussy began their death struggle. On March 14, 1864, the Federal army assaulted the small fort. After three attempts to scale the fort, overpowering forces finally overwhelmed the defenders. Everyone in the fort was killed, wounded, or captured. For the next few weeks the rest of the regiment, along with Taylor's army, would be retreating before the combined forces of Banks.[127]

Walker's Texas Division in turn served as the rearguard for Taylor's army for much of the march toward Shreveport. The division was under constant threat of attack from harassing Federal cavalry. On one occasion the division set up an ambush and wounded several of the enemy and routed the remainder. All in all, however, the retreat proved to be dispiriting.[128] Religion became very important to the troops, who understood they might soon be facing a major battle.[129] After seeing their comrades left behind at Fort DeRussy to face the ultimate challenge, the Texans knew that their turn might be fast approaching from the south. Facing death in the upcoming showdown with Banks, the men held revivals in the camps and tried to make their peace with God.[130]

In early April, the Union army began to close in on the retreating Confederates and General Walker announced to his troops "that it now became a race between [his] men and those of the enemy, who should get to Pleasant Hill [a town on the Stage Coach Road about forty miles south of Shreveport] first."[131] On April 8, 1864, the day that the Confederate army had long prepared for finally arrived. Taylor ordered Walker to march his division toward the small Louisiana town of Mansfield, where the Union lead elements were arriving piecemeal. The Nineteenth Texas, as part of Scurry's Third Brigade, was formed into a battle line on the south side of the Stage Road.[132]

The Confederates waited for the Federals to attack, but the enemy had not brought up enough men to challenge Taylor's army. At 4:00 p.m. on April 8, Taylor ordered an assault on the Federal right. Shortly afterward, Walker ordered his Texans forward. The Union line immediately began to crumble. After such a long retreat, the Texas troops were more than ready to fight. The blue line disintegrated before the onslaught due to Banks' inability to bring enough of his troops into action. Union troops began to retreat south to the town of Pleasant Hill, a small community fifteen miles south of Mansfield. As they ran down the road, they threw away anything that might slow them down. Their muskets, knapsacks, and haversacks, among other items, were "literally strewn" down on the path toward Pleasant Hill.[133] General Taylor's victory was complete. Much of the lead elements of the Federal army had been routed or captured, and now General Banks had to save the rest of it.[134]

The next day the tired Confederate army pursued the Federals retreating down the road to Pleasant Hill. Banks had decided to make a stand there, and Taylor was ready to attack. About 4:00 p.m. on April 9, the battle began when the right wing of Taylor's army attacked strong positions of artillery supported by infantry. These Arkansas and Missouri troops, commanded by Brig. Gen. Thomas J. Churchill, were unable to pierce the enemy line and fell back into the ranks of Walker's Texans. The Nineteenth Texas, as part of Scurry's brigade, stood in the direct line of retreat of Churchill's men. Counter-attacking Federals were closely pursuing the grey-clad troops. Eventually, the entirety of the forces became intermingled in a bloody death struggle. While attempting to pull back from the chaos of the hand-to-hand fighting, the Nineteenth Texas lost its regimental colors.[135]

Many years after the conflict, a veteran of the battle who had served in Company E of the Nineteenth Texas, Pvt. Henry C. Joiner, posed a question to his old comrades *via* the *Confederate*

Veteran asking whether anyone knew exactly what had happened and who had taken the banner. Joiner recounted his story. While under orders for a general retreat, he remembered that the color bearer, Jim Crossland, (Compiled Service Records indicate that either Joiner's memory had faded or that 'R. R. Crossland' was nicknamed 'Jim' due to the absence of a soldier record for 'Jim Crossland') had been badly wounded and left on the field. An unidentified member of Company F had picked up the colors and had carried them toward the rear of the battle lines. Joiner saw the colors closely behind him, but when the regiment reformed they were missing. The men had left their color bearer too far behind and he was captured along with the flag, likely by the One-hundredth and Nineteenth Illinois Infantry. In his report of the battle, Union Col. William F. Lynch wrote, "the One hundred and nineteenth Illinois...advanced on the enemy, keeping the left on the field. They drove before them a Texas regiment, the colors of which they captured."[136]

While the loss of the colors was disheartening, Colonel Waterhouse was once again singled out for his exceptional ability at leading his regiment in battle. With the Confederate line collapsing all around him, Waterhouse rallied his troops to prepare for a counterattack. General Taylor wrote in his official report of the battle,

> Churchill in his attack did not gain ground enough to his right or use his cavalry efficiently. The consequence was that...the enemy outflanked his right and threw him into much conduction. Brigadier-

General Scurry...behaved most
nobly, and speaks highly of Colonel
Waterhouse.[137]

The retreat from the chaotic struggle near the
center of the Confederate line was the only action
that the Nineteenth Texas saw that disappointing
day. The battle ended with neither side achieving
what was actually intended, but the Federal army
under General Banks did continue its retreat
afterwards. The regiment of Texans, as a part of
Taylor's army, had accomplished the strategic goal of
ridding central Louisiana of Federal troops.[138]

Immediately after the fight at Pleasant Hill,
General E. Kirby Smith, as the commander of Trans-
Mississippi Department, told Waterhouse's
regiment, as part of Walker's division, to prepare to
march into Arkansas to assist in turning back
Federal Maj. Gen. General Frederick Steele in his
advance on Shreveport from the north. Before
moving out, the men were allowed to rest near their
previous camp at Mansfield for a few days. After
this short break, the troops, once again, would be on
an extended campaign traveling roughly fifteen
miles a day.[139]

On April 15, 1864, the Nineteenth Texas
marched for Shreveport. The regiment passed
through that town and then proceeded east toward
Minden, Louisiana. Close to the Arkansas border,
the regiment received a long overdue payday. Along
the way, residents came out and cheered the men.
The Confederate victories in the vicinity prompted
the local populace to show their appreciation to the
troops and cheered the grey-clad soldiers at every

town along the way. On April 26 the weary Texas troops arrived in the vicinity of Camden, Arkansas, where the invader had occupied fortified entrenchments. General Steele, thinking that his position was untenable began withdrawing his troops on April 26. Not realizing that the Federals were abandoning their works, the Confederates quickly attempted to catch their foes before they reached the safety of Little Rock. The Texans thus prepared for their third engagement in less than a month.[140]

The sound of musketry awoke the men of the Nineteenth Texas at midnight on April 30. The Federals had been caught crossing the Saline River and seemed to be in a precarious situation. Although the outlook for the Federals appeared bleak, General Steele was lucky to have a natural defensive line flanked by impassable swamps that firmly anchored his flanks. He would also be assisted by the poorly planned and executed efforts of the Confederates to attack him.[141]

Undaunted by the possibilities of another Pleasant Hill-like frontal assault, Kirby Smith ordered his men forward. Waterhouse formed his regiment on the right end of the Confederate line and pushed through the small field directly into a murderous fire from the well-protected Yankees. Walker's Texas Division lost more men in this senseless charge than in any other engagement of the war. The Confederates continued their assault until they were exhausted. General Steele quickly pulled his army to safety on the other side of the river as soon as the attacks ended. During one of the charges, General Scurry was mortally wounded. The popular brigade commander died the next day. That night in camp, the men of his Third Brigade were in a somber mood. They loved Scurry and were loath to see him killed before their eyes in a senseless charge. Afterward, the Texas troops marched into the small town of Tulip, escorting the remains of General Scurry, to bury him with military honors.[142]

Unlike previous engagements, the after-action reports of the battle do not contain specific casualties from either Union or Confederate commanders. The confused situation of Walker's Division and the speedy withdrawal of the Federal army likely affected the ability of the officers to accurately record the names of the killed, wounded, and missing. According to estimates, Steele suffered fewer than 800 casualties, while Kirby Smith lost approximately 1,000 men in his frontal assaults. The Nineteenth Texas was fortunate enough to record its losses, which included ten killed and eighteen wounded. Three original members of Company A, two privates and Maj. William L. Crawford (the former company commander), were counted among the wounded.[143]

After the Battle of Jenkins' Ferry and the retreat of the Federal army, Kirby Smith released the division from Arkansas and ordered the Texans, once again, to Louisiana.[144] The division retraced its steps it had taken the previous month. While en route, the Nineteenth Texas had a significant change in leadership take place. Colonel Waterhouse, the beloved regimental commander, was promoted to brigadier general and selected to lead Scurry's brigade. Waterhouse's promotion was no surprise to the men of the regiment. The colonel had been in the thick of the fighting in every engagement, and he had been singled out for bravery at both Milliken's Bend and Mansfield. Even though the men would miss him, they would be placed in the very capable hands of the newly promoted Col. Ennis Ward Taylor. After another hard march, the regiment reached Alexandria and camped near the spot where they had begun the previous campaign. Unfortunately for General Taylor, the Greyhounds had reached him too late to be of use because the Federal army under Banks had escaped.[145]

After such a grueling season of fighting, the Nineteenth Texas Infantry settled down for a well-deserved rest at Pineville, Louisiana.[146] The break did not last long, however, and the division packed up once again and moved east on the 4th of June. During this march, the division was again affected by a major change in command. General Walker, the leader of the Greyhounds, was assigned to command the District of Western Louisiana, formerly headed by Taylor, who was promoted to lieutenant general and given command of a district that included east Louisiana, Mississippi, and Alabama. While the Confederates' spirits were good after the successful campaign against the Federal invaders, the Texans had exhausted their supplies and were a ragged bunch. Lt. Col. William H. Redwood, of the Sixteenth Texas Infantry, a sister regiment to the Nineteenth Texas Infantry, wrote a public letter to the citizens of Texas that read, in part, "The army of Louisiana is ragged and barefoot; winter is approaching…your homes are safe, but the soldiers will suffer, unless clothing is prepared for them." But even though the Texans were a ragged bunch, they would soon be on the march again.[147]

Gen. Braxton Bragg, as military advisor to President Jefferson Davis, decided that the military threat to the Trans-Mississippi Department was no longer imminent and issued orders to transfer most of the troops there to the armies east of the Mississippi River during August 1864.[148] The Nineteenth Texas, as part of the veteran Greyhound Division, was ordered east as well. The regiment reached the banks of the Mississippi River, near Harrisonburg, but due to gunboat patrols it was unable to make the crossing.[149] After a change in orders, the regiment marched back into Arkansas, under the temporary command of Maj. Gen. John B. Magruder. At Monticello, the division participated in a formal review for the commanding general.[150] In October, the Texans returned to Camden, Arkansas where they had camped a few months earlier after the withdrawal of General Steele. The Confederates were put to work building fortifications to defend against another possible invasion from Little Rock. The regiment moved closer to the Federal supply lines on the Red River in mid-November, and then proceeded to its winter camp in Louisiana on the road between Minden and Shreveport.[151]

In the spring of 1865, the division was alerted by Walker, commanding the Texas district, that Federals under the command of Maj. Gen. Edward R. S. Canby were on the move as part of yet another invasion attempt to capture Texas. Upon hearing the news and receiving orders to counter this threat, the Nineteenth Texas marched back into Texas for the first time in almost three years.[152] The division marched into Texas in two separate wings; both taking different roads from the Mansfield, Louisiana. Their destination was Crockett, Texas, where both parts would converge and the leadership would assess the situation before issuing further orders. While the regiment was on the move to protect the state of Texas, General Robert E. Lee was surrendering at Appomattox Court House. The war had been lost in the east, and without Lee's Army of Northern Virginia, other Confederate armies in the field began to capitulate.[153]

During this time of confusion, the regiment camped near Hempstead, Texas, at the Liendo Plantation in April 1865. Due to their extended campaigns, the men were short on many items that brought them comfort in camp. Items such as paper, ink, and tobacco were procured from friendly merchants in Houston and provided to the men at no charge. After news of the surrender reached the Texans, men began to leave the camp one by one. The Greyhounds did not take part in a formal surrender of their own; instead, many made their way back to the families they had left in 1862. Meanwhile, the Nineteenth Texas Volunteer Infantry did not simply disband and walk away. Under the leadership of Col. Ennis Ward Taylor, the regiment marched north and disbanded the men by companies as each company approached its hometown. The final destination was Jefferson, Texas, where Taylor broke ranks with Company A for the last time of the war. Before releasing the company, Taylor delivered a brief speech and admonished the men to be good citizens just as they had been good soldiers in the division. It was a solemn occasion, with tears filling the men's eyes as they bid their comrades farewell.[154]

The Nineteenth Texas Infantry was in perhaps the hardest marching division in the entire Confederate army covering more than 3,500 miles in just three years of service.[155] The men of the regiment, while still stationed hundreds of miles away from their families, had the desirable situation of being able to defend their home state as well as their loved ones from Union aggression in the area. The Nineteenth Texas accomplished this in four major battles and several other skirmishes. Without the division of Greyhounds that was raised in 1862, it is doubtful that General Taylor would have been able to fend off the invasion of General Banks' army.[156] Similarly, General Steele's invasion was stopped just weeks later by the same troops after marching 175 miles to participate in that campaign. Undoubtedly, the Nineteenth Texas made a definite impact on the war, and probably helped prolong the short life of the Confederate States of America.

Lt. Gen. Richard Taylor
Photo source: Sons of Confederate Veterans
http://www.scvtaylorcamp.com/Dick%20Taylor.ht
ml

Pvt. William M. Hogsett
Company C, 19th Texas Infantry

CHAPTER 4

"Go to Your Homes and Make True and Devoted Citizens"

Company A disbanded, along with the remainder of the Nineteenth Texas Infantry, after two years and eleven months in the field. The members of the company, along with the rest of Walker's Texas Division, claimed to go home undefeated. Though their service record does not necessarily validate this claim, they had served in some of the Trans-Mississippi's greatest campaigns. These Texans held the distinction of being the first Confederates to face black troops in combat during the American Civil War, had participated in blocking the greatest offensive in the region during the Red River Campaign of 1864, and had marched to the relief of Arkansas just a few days after fighting two pitched battles on consecutive days in central Louisiana. Marching more than 3,500 miles in less than three years, the Texans were one of the most respected military units in the Confederacy's Trans-Mississippi Department, which frequently had regional commanders struggling to bring their troops into operations against the enemy. After the company marched back to Jefferson in the late spring of 1865, the former soldiers would attempt to rebuild the lives they had left in the spring of 1862, facing endless challenges along the way.[157]

Records indicate that fourteen members of the company died during the war, though miraculously none died in combat. Thirteen men died of disease, while one, Pvt. Jefferson E. Dale, was executed for desertion. Of those men who perished during the conflict, only three were identified in the 1860 census and they were all listed as farmers. Through three years of hard marching and fighting, most of the men in Company A endured unimaginable suffering, and then, in April 1865, the Confederate defeat became, possibly, the most difficult situation to cope with. The survivors made their way home to begin the next chapter of their lives.[158]

While thirty-five percent of the men in Company A, or twenty-four members, are found in the United States Census of 1860, only twenty-five percent of the survivors are found in 1870. There are multiple explanations for this, including the inefficiency of the census-takers and the general distrust of the Federal government by ex-Confederates who were hiding from the government employees of the Reconstruction government. Based upon the available data, it appears that about half of the men of Company A returned to their pre-war counties after the war. Of those that moved elsewhere, eighty percent migrated to urban areas, with half of them relocating west and the other half moving east to Louisiana and Mississippi. Many more of those that marched home would find themselves migrating west in their later years, with only twenty-five percent remaining in their pre-war county by 1890.[159]

Among the men returning to their pre-war homes was Brig. Gen. Richard Waterhouse. His wife and child were waiting for his return to Jefferson so he could rebuild his family business. In the years leading up to the war, the young man had expanded his and his father's business, "R. Waterhouse and Son," to Jefferson from San Augustine. Heavily invested in the mercantile business, Jefferson was the logical choice for the Waterhouse family due to its prominence as the most commercialized city in north Texas. It was while the Waterhouses were moving to the new town that the threat of war loomed over the country. Both of the Waterhouses had fought in the Mexican War, the younger man as a teenage runaway. Richard Waterhouse Sr. had later become a prominent Texas politician, serving as representative in the state assembly twice, being elected in 1857 and 1859, therefore it is likely that his son had political motivations when he began lobbying for a commission to raise an infantry regiment that was eventually mustered into service in May 1862.[160]

After the war, Richard Waterhouse returned to his home with limited resources. He had written to his father about selling his mercantile in Jefferson, a sale that very likely took place in 1863. Sadly, Waterhouse's father was murdered in San Augustine in December of 1863, shortly after selling his Jefferson mercantile operation to an acquaintance in town. The death of his father deprived the son of his business partner and mentor.

Waterhouse would have to rebuild his financial empire with nothing but the cash from his previous enterprises.[161]

Fearful of being prosecuted by the United States government, Waterhouse returned to his home in Jefferson and packed for his escape into Mexico. He travelled to Matamoros, Mexico, where he made contact with William Henry Wallace, a family friend and business associate from San Augustine. In a letter to Wallace, Waterhouse writes vaguely, perhaps fearing that his letter might fall into the wrong hands. He says he has been detained by "circumstances which could not be controlled" and explains that he will go to Mexico City to await word from him regarding the situation in Texas.[162] Many Confederate troops crossed into Mexico to join the forces of the French Empire, and it is highly likely that Waterhouse was assessing the situation for himself. Waterhouse was also considering his prospects of starting a business in the country, noting the labor market and the unstable government. Although the letter does not survive, sometime after January 1866, Waterhouse returned home. He received a pardon from President Andrew Johnson on October 15, 1866, which gave him the assurance of his personal safety.[163]

After returning to Jefferson, Waterhouse was very busy trying to determine how he could recover from his family's economic losses incurred during the war. With the loss of his store and his family's slaves, compounded by the investment losses incurred with the collapse of Confederate currency, his future seemed uncertain. In any event,

Waterhouse was able to return to the dry goods mercantile business. He also ventured into land speculation, which was very taxing on the former general and required him to travel extensively across the state. There is no record of what happened to Rose, Waterhouse's wife, whom he wrote so often during the wartime years; however, his ten-year old son and namesake, Richard, was living with Waterhouse's close family friend and attorney, William Henry Wallace, in 1870, possibly due to the death of his wife.[164]

In March 1876, Waterhouse was travelling between his land holdings in Jefferson, San Augustine, and San Antonio. While staying in a hotel in Waco, Texas, he took a serious fall down a flight of stairs. His fall resulted in his contraction of a severe case of pneumonia and resulted in his death on March 20 at age forty-four.[165] Waterhouse's body was sent home, and he was interred in Oakwood Cemetery in Jefferson.[166]

Miranda W. Covey, who also returned to Jefferson, had enlisted in Company A as a second lieutenant and was brevetted to first lieutenant during the war. Covey, originally from Georgia, had moved to Jefferson before the war and started a small farm. Covey became a community leader and was elected as a delegate to the Democratic National Convention in 1860. At the war's end, he returned to Jefferson and married Susan A. Gannt, a recent arrival from Arkansas, with whom he rebuilt his farm and started a family. With a wife and three children, Covey maintained a humble existence until his death on April 21, 1884, when he was laid to rest next to many of his comrades in arms at Oakwood Cemetery in Jefferson, Texas.[167]

Richard Smithson had emigrated from England to Texas with his brother, William, and his sister, Mary Ann. Smithson moved to Jefferson before the war where he lived with Shadrach Eggers, the owner of the *Herald and Gazette* newspaper. Eggers boarded four young men with his family, including Smithson, perhaps as part of their salary as printers in his employ. The newspaper man had combined the *Jefferson Gazette* with the *Jefferson Herald*, the other Jefferson newspaper in 1858. Smithson was working for Eggers in this capacity when the first shots were fired at Fort Sumter in 1861. Leaving his promising career in 1862, Smithson joined Company A of the Nineteenth Texas Infantry and served for the duration of the war, enduring sickness and multiple stays in the hospital.[168]

Smithson's records after the war are incomplete, but it is clear that he returned home to Jefferson and shared a room with three other employees while he resumed his newspaper career. In 1878, he fathered a child that would be named for him, but fate called to him to an early grave at age thirty-four years old in that same year. In 1880 his child was living with William A. Cossart and his wife, who listed the two-year old Richard Smithson as their own son. Smithson was buried, like many of his comrades, in Jefferson's Oakwood Cemetery.[169]

Waterhouse, Covey, and Smithson represent those soldiers in Company A that returned home to rebuild their shattered lives and maintained an allegiance to their pre-war home counties. Others soldiers returned to their pre-war counties and then found exciting opportunities in different urban centers, mostly in Dallas and Fort Worth. Some of these men would become important leaders in their new communities of Dallas and Fort Worth. Many of Company A's youthful officers became enterprising businessmen in the Reconstruction years, overcoming the challenges presented to them by their government and building wealthy estates across the Dallas/Fort Worth Metroplex. William J. Clark, the Crawford brothers, and Ennis W. Taylor became financial tycoons of the Gilded Age and helped build what would become two of the largest cities in Texas.

Clark, who commanded Company A from 1863 through the end of the war, returned home, packed his belongings, and moved to Dallas, as did several of his former mess mates. To support his wife and three sons he ventured into the mercantile business, likely influenced by his wartime commander, Waterhouse, with whom he had served for three years. After moving to Dallas, his business quickly became very successful and his net worth catapulted him into becoming the wealthiest former member of Company A with more than $80,000.00 worth of property in 1870. With his three sons following him into business and a servant to help keep house, Clark made his fortune. He eventually retired, leaving his business to his children, and lived a long life, dying at the age of seventy-three in 1901. He was buried in Dallas' Greenwood Cemetery, where he rests with his wife and other members of his family.[170]

William L. Crawford, Clark's predecessor as the original commander of Company A, and his brother Meriwether L. Crawford (known by his initials "M.L.") also moved to Dallas after the war. Originally from Estill County in Kentucky, the brothers both studied law in the years leading up to the Civil War but joined the war effort before they were admitted to the bar. After the conclusion of the war, William was quickly admitted to the Texas State Bar and opened a law practice in Jefferson. M.L. moved to Galveston, where he clerked for a law office while finishing his legal studies. M.L. was admitted to the Texas bar in 1870 and returned to Jefferson shortly thereafter. Partnering in Jefferson for the next ten years, the brothers eventually decided to relocate their office in Dallas in 1880.[171]

During M.L. Crawford's post-war career he was a highly respected politician and war veteran. He was elected judge for the Fifth Judicial District of Texas in 1872, a position he held until his death, while at times performing additional duties, many of which focused on community service. In 1877, M.L. was selected as a regent for the new University of Texas. During the hotly contested Democratic National Convention of 1896, Crawford attended as a gold-standard-supporting delegate. In 1897 he was appointed a national committee member of the Indianapolis Monetary Convention, which had a strong influence on President William McKinley and his administration's decision resulting in the Gold Standard Act of 1900. On May 15, 1910, after a lifetime of achievements, M.L. Crawford died at the age of sixty-nine years. His brother, who also contributed greatly to his community, would outlive him by another ten years.[172]

William L. Crawford's career also placed him in the state and national spotlights as well, in some cases right next to his younger brother. Crawford was also a brilliant attorney; one colleague called him "the ablest nisi prius lawyer that ever lived."[173] He undoubtedly had a colorful career, serving as a delegate to the Constitutional Convention of Texas in 1875, one term in the Texas House of Representatives, multiple times as a delegate to the Texas State Democratic Convention, two terms on the Democratic National Convention, and one time as a delegate to the United States Electoral College in 1896. Crawford, like his brother M.L., was a strong supporter of the gold standard, an issue that caused dissention within the Democratic Party. Even with his strong stand for gold, he was able to maintain his popularity within the party and was greatly admired by his colleagues and constituents alike. Survived by three sons and a daughter, William L. Crawford died on February 17, 1920, at the age of eighty-two.[174]

Ennis W. Taylor joined Company A as a private in 1862 but was elected major of the Nineteenth Texas Infantry just a week after the regiment organized. Taylor had immigrated with his family to Texas in 1846. With very little schooling, young Ennis worked in a variety of agricultural pursuits before getting a job with a druggist in Jefferson in 1855. He quickly displayed his determination to succeed in life by completing his studies with the United States Dispensatory in eighteen months. Partnering with his employer, he opened a second drug store, where he made $6,000.00 in his nineteenth year, an immense amount of money for a teenager in 1860. His civilian career, however, would be put on hold for the next four years as he dedicated his time to serving the Confederacy in a variety of ways, culminating with his promotion to colonel of the Nineteenth Texas, following Waterhouse's promotion to brigade commander. When the end of the war came, it was Taylor that maintained order within the command, personally marching the men back to their home communities. When he formed the regiment the for last time, he told the men "the war is now over...you have been true and brave soldiers...go to your homes and make true and devoted citizens, as you have been soldiers of your country."[175] With little more than pride, he returned to Jefferson to rebuild his career and pre-war life.[176]

Taylor was immensely successful in Jefferson, where he maintained his pharmacy, served as mayor, invested and promoted railroads, and became a town promoter and builder. Taylor also chaired the local Confederate veterans' organization, which met regularly in town. Taylor with a close friend, former Col. W. M. Harrison, became the founders and owners of East Line & Red River Railroad, which was built from Jefferson to Sulphur Springs, Texas. This line was sold to railroad magnate Jay Gould for a profit of $120,000.00, quite a feat for inexperienced railroad men. After developing this Texas route, Taylor shifted his efforts to building a line from Seligman, Missouri to Eureka Springs, Arkansas. While building the line, he began investing in Eureka Springs' natural springs as a medical wonder and built the Crescent Hotel, which became a resort and spa for the wealthy people of the Gilded Age.[177]

In 1888, Taylor moved his family to Tarrant County, Texas, where he settled in Fort Worth. Here he maintained a drug store under the management of his son-in-law, Charles Connery, and ventured into capital investments, banking, and philanthropy. He lived a very comfortable life in Fort Worth in a large home with the assistance of two live-in African- American servants. He donated enormous sums of money to his church, the First United Methodist Church, as well as the United Benevolent Association, a state chartered insurance program for the indigent. Serving as a leading member of the United Confederate Veterans, Taylor worked closely with K. M. Van Zandt until his death on April 3, 1908. Ennis Ward Taylor was buried in the historic Oakwood Cemetery of Fort Worth.[178]

While half of the company's traceable veterans moved west to Tarrant and Dallas counties, many members also moved due to economic opportunity but remained closer to their pre-war homes. The data of course is incomplete, but approximately twenty-five percent of the men with surviving records show that they moved to neighboring areas fairly close to their previous homes. These men tended to move less than one hundred miles away from their pre-war counties. With the end of the war, Texas became the fastest growing ex-Confederate state and opportunities for ex-soldiers increased, mostly toward the central part of the state.

Capt. Aaron C. Smith initially returned home to Jefferson before leaving for other opportunities in the region. Smith was a successful merchant in Jefferson before the war, not unlike several others in Company A. It was due to his fantastic capabilities as an organizer and bookkeeper in private life that led to his appointment as the assistant quartermaster for the regiment. His talents were quickly noted and he was promoted to brigade quartermaster, a highly demanding job requiring the ability to keep over 2,500 men supplied with clothing, equipment, and food.[179]

After the war, Smith emulated many of his peers by moving his business enterprises out of Jefferson. By 1880, Smith had moved his general store to Queen City in Cass County, about thirty miles north of Jefferson. His business was phenomenally successful, resulting in his acquisition of a comfortable homestead that included five children, one maid, and two butlers with room left for a local music teacher that stayed as a boarder. Death was all too common in Smith's life as it took his wife, Elizabeth, from him far too soon. Eventually he remarried, this time to a Pennsylvania girl by the name of Caroline. She came with a child and by the time he was seventy-two they had two grandchildren living in their home. It is quite possible that Caroline's child had also succumbed to the frailty of life that was common in nineteenth century America. Smith's second wife also died and left him to die a lonely death on August 2, 1925, at the age of eighty-nine.[180]

Henry McLaughlin was only seventeen when he joined Company A of the Nineteenth Texas

Infantry. He was working hard at an early age as a farmhand before he enlisted. In 1860 he was living with a middle-aged widow and several other young men who were also assisting the lady with work on her farm in Milam County. His Confederate service record indicates that he was admitted to the hospital on at least two occasions; however, he appears to have served until the end of the war. After the war, Henry moved to Austin County, again working as a farmer and living with another large family. By 1880, he had married and started his own farm back in Milam County. Henry raised two children, a boy and a girl, before his death in 1887 at the age of forty-three.[181]

Some men left Marion County, likely to avoid the sting of dishonor from their Confederate service. Soldiers made important connections, networking with many powerful people in the service. Many Confederate officers and enlisted men would be elected to powerful positions or become business leaders in their respective communities. Those men who had poor service records would often find themselves at a disadvantage in their social and business lives. Capt. A.R.K. Northrop and Pvt. Marshall N. Dale left Texas after the war, possibly to put their war record behind them.

A.R.K. Northrop originally joined Company A of the Nineteenth Texas Infantry as a private before he was transferred to Company E as a Second Lieutenant. Northrop was born in Louisiana and had moved before the war to San Augustine, where he boarded with a silversmith who employed him. He quickly moved up the ranks and became commander of his new company in February 1863 after Capt. Felix B. Dixon resigned due to poor eyesight. A.R.K. Northrop then resigned his command in May 1864, after the regiment had fought its three great battles, at the request of Colonel Waterhouse due to his "inability to control or command his company in the presence of the enemy."[182] After the war, Northrop, possibly escaping the sting of dishonor, moved to Mississippi where he became a successful dentist and reared a large family with seven children.[183]

The Dale brothers, Marshall N. and Jefferson E., enlisted into the Nineteenth Texas Infantry, Company A, from Titus County, west of Jefferson, Texas. Both men had earlier joined the Texas state militia as part of the Eighth Brigade in July of 1861, during the initial rush to arms after Fort Sumter and Manassas.[184] The Dale brothers arrived in Jefferson likely after reading in local newspapers about the regiment's formation. Life at Camp Waterhouse must have been very strenuous for the newly arrived farm boys, as the transition to military life would result in serious consequences for the Dale family. Military drill from sun up to sun down was new to men who had prior service in a militia unit that had little if any military discipline. Not only did the men suffer from the daily drill and military hardships, by the time the brothers arrived in Arkansas they were both listed as sick.[185]

The brothers were lucky to survive their illness. During the regiment's service, 127 men died from disease, with ninety-one percent of those deaths occurring before the men left Arkansas. But their luck would not last long. Ignoring their orders and deserting their posts, the brothers packed and left for Texas in February 1863. They were quickly caught and given courts-martial, resulting in death penalty convictions for both men. Jefferson E. Dale was brought before the regiment, where his brother watched the deadly work of the firing squad. In a twist of fate, Pres. Jefferson Davis pardoned Marshall N. Dale before he was executed. Ignoring the fact that desertion was not taken lightly, Marshall stubbornly ran away again on September 6, 1863, this time from the Texan camp at Bayou Cotile, Louisiana. Making his way back to Titus County, where he remained in hiding for the duration of the war. After the war, with the return of the Texas veterans to the state, Marshall left the state and made his way to Washington County, Arkansas. Here he farmed and raised a family, leaving behind his tainted record of service for the Confederacy. He left no record of his later years and it is unclear if he ever returned to Texas after 1870.[186]

A great many members of Company A left behind incomplete records or no records at all. While many officers and men became business and community leaders, an equal number managed to avoid contact with the government and left very little evidence of their post-war years. Most of these men worked as farmers and were missed by the census takers, and most Texas counties did not record births and deaths until the twentieth century.

Among those men was Finley M. Morgan, a poor farmer before the war. He had, like most of his fellow soldiers, immigrated to Texas from another southern state before the war, his home state being North Carolina. Morgan had enlisted as a private but quickly attained the rank of sergeant. Although he was absent without leave for a short period during the summer of 1863, he returned to his company and served throughout the rest of the war. Returning home, he went back to the farm and married a North Carolina native by the name of Mary. Unfortunately, there is no further record of what happened to him after 1870. Like so many of the other members of the company, he left no record of his later years.[187]

Sixty-five percent of the men who served with Company A have either missing or incomplete records. This gap in information is unfortunate for those attempting a detailed report for their post-war lives. Approximately one-half of these men have left some records that give the researcher some basic data to indicate their activity during at least one census from 1870 to 1880. Of these men studied, two-thirds verifiably moved from one county to another in their post-war years. Pvt. James Armstrong moved to Austin County after the war and became a hide trader in the area west of Houston. His record after 1870 is unknown. Pvt. John Burk left his home county of Buchanan and moved to Erath County. Here on the Texas frontier he farmed with his family until at least 1880, after which he disappears from records. Pvt. O. A. Mathews returned to Marion County only to move to Hunt County, where he was farming in 1870 while raising a family. He is not found in the subsequent records. J. F. Smith and J. F. Taylor were farming in Upshur and Harrison Counties respectively before the war. They were both found to have returned to their home counties in the 1870 census, but neither one was located after that year.[188]

Many men of Company A made an indelible mark on the state of Texas in the years following the war. While some of the men cannot be traced, Company A produced lawyers, doctors, pharmacists, clerks, entrepreneurs, merchants, laborers, farmers, railroad promoters, and even state legislators. Many of these men became leaders while others stepped back into their anonymous pre-war lives. While their service in the Confederate army was undoubtedly the defining moment of their lives, these men continued to make history and rebuild their shattered dreams.

Unknown Confederate Veterans in Jefferson, Texas in 1902
Photo source: Marion County TX GenWeb
http://www.rootsweb.ancestry.com/~txmarion/resources/Photos.html

Conclusion

In 1988, Gary Canada, a historian and reenactor of the American Civil War, formed a living history organization dedicated to preserving the memory of the Texans that formed the Nineteenth Texas Infantry more than a century earlier. His new organization was named "Company A, Nineteenth Texas Volunteer Infantry." Colonel Canada, as he was known to those in the reenacting community, passed away before he could complete his long-term goal of writing an exhaustive regimental history. While he did not finish that work, in his efforts to research his beloved regiment, he compiled a collection of historical materials that would lead to further attempts by later historians to fulfill his objective. While this effort does not fulfill his objective, it does build upon his efforts by focusing on the one company that attracted his attention because it stood out among its sister companies within the regiment.

Company A performed admirably on the field and achieved a remarkable record. The company, while its experience paralleled that of the other nine companies in the regiment, maintained its distinction as a diverse, hard-fighting unit that gained praise from its brigade and divisional

86

commanders on at least two occasions. Service records indicate that multiple men from the company were recognized for their exceptional qualities and placed in extremely powerful positions within the regiment and brigade. Their accomplishments during and after the war reflect the unique status of the company to which they belonged.

Capt. William L. Crawford, the only college educated man in the company, was eventually promoted to major. After the war, he and his brother, Pvt. M. L. Crawford, became prominent attorneys in Dallas. William Crawford also became the only member of the regiment that was elected to the Texas legislature in the post-war years. Second Lieutenant Miranda W. Covey, who had served in the 1860 Democratic National Convention, rose from private to the position of company quartermaster. Capt. Aaron C. Smith, a wealthy merchant before the war who became the brigade quartermaster, continued his pre-war success in the mercantile business. His wealth produced an impressive estate employing three servants and a live-in music teacher for his children. Perhaps as a testament to their commander, these men adhered to the immortal words of Col. Ennis Ward Taylor when he admonished the men to become as good as citizens as they had been as soldiers.

Today, the Nineteenth Texas Infantry lives on as a living history regiment that attempts to carry on the mission for which it was founded. This author serves as an executive officer within that organization and has attempted to bring life to the historical account of Company A. Every year the reactivated Company A can be found on the streets of Jefferson in its humble attempt to inform, educate, and entertain the public about Texas's unique contribution to the "Lost Cause" of the Confederacy.

NOTES

INTRODUCTION

[1] Bell I. Wiley, *The Life of Johnny Reb: The Common Soldier of the Confederacy* (Baton Rouge: Louisiana State University Press, 1943), 22-25.

[2] Shelby Foote, *The Civil War: A Narrative, Fort Sumter to Perryville* (New York: Random House, 1958), 60-61.

[3] Charles David Grear, *Why Texans Fought in the Civil War* (College Station: Texas A & M University Press, 2010), 1-9.

[4] James M. McPherson, *Battle Cry of Freedom: The Civil War Era* (New York: Oxford University Press, 1988), 39-41.

[5] Ralph Wooster, *Texas and Texans in the Civil War* (Austin: Eakin Press, 1995), 31, 105, 119; Randolph B. Campbell, *Gone to Texas: A History of the Lone Star State* (New York: Oxford University Press, 2003), 207-209.

[6] Grear, *Why Texans Fought in the Civil War*, 5-9.

[7] Fred Tarpley, *Jefferson: Riverport to the Southwest* (Wolfe City, TX: Henington Publishing Company, 1983), 49-57.

[8] Russell F. Weigley, *The American Way of War* (Bloomington: Indiana University Press, 1967), 97; McPherson, *Battle Cry of Freedom*, 472-477; John K. Mahon, "Civil War Infantry Assault Tactics," *Military Affairs* 25 (Summer 1961), 57-68; Allen R. Millet and Peter Maslowski. *For the Common Defense: A Military History of the United States of America* (New York: Free Press, 1994), 237.

CHAPTER ONE

[9] Ralph Wooster, *Texas and Texans in the Civil War* (Austin: Eakin Press, 1995), 31.

[10] Stephen A. Dupree, *Planting the Union Flag in Texas: The Campaigns of Major General Nathaniel P. Banks in the West* (College Station: Texas A&M University Press, 2008), 27-37.

[11] Ludwell H. Johnson, "Fort Sumter and Confederate Diplomacy," *The Journal of Southern History* 26 (Nov. 1960), 441-477.

[12] Paul M. Angle, "Lincoln's Power with Words," *Papers of the Abraham Lincoln Association* 3 (1981), 8-27.

[13] Wooster, *Texas and Texans in the Civil War*, 25.

[14] Ibid., 21-24.

[15] Wooster, *Texas and Texans in the Civil War*, 25-34; Richard B. McCaslin, *Fighting Stock: John S. "Rip" Ford of Texas* (Fort Worth: Texas Christian University Press, 2011), 122-131; Randolph B. Campbell, *Gone to Texas: A History of the Lone Star State* (Oxford: Oxford University Press, 2003), 246-248; Thomas W. Cutrer, *Ben McCulloch and the Frontier Military Tradition* (Chapel Hill: University of North Carolina Press, 1993), 177-190.

[16] Wooster, *Texas and Texans in the Civil War*, 52-57; James M. McPherson, *Battle Cry of Freedom: The Civil War Era* (Oxford: Oxford University Press, 1988), 392-427.

[17] Richard Lowe, *Walker's Texas Division, C.S.A.: Greyhounds of the Trans-Mississippi* (Baton Rouge: Louisiana State University Press, 2006), 4-5.

[18] Wooster, *Texas and Texans in the Civil War*, 27-33; McCaslin, *Fighting Stock*, 133; Albert Burton Moore, *Conscription and Conflict in the Confederacy* (Columbia: University of South Carolina Press, 1924), xvi.

[19] Joseph P. Blessington, *The Campaigns of Walker's Texas Division: By a Private Soldier* (Austin: Pemberton Press, 1968), 10.

[20] Randolph B. Campbell and Richard G. Lowe, *Wealth and Power in Antebellum Texas* (College Station: Texas A & M University Press, 1977), 60-61; United States Department of the Interior, Bureau of the Census, Eighth Census, 1860, Texas [Marion and Harrison Counties] Record Group 29, National Archives, Washington, D.C., (hereafter cited as U.S. Census with appropriate decade and county designation); Colonel Richard Waterhouse, Jr. to Rose Waterhouse, May 22, 1864, Richard Waterhouse, Jr., Letters, 1858-1872, University of Arkansas at Little Rock Institute for History and Culture, Little Rock, Arkansas.

[21] Campbell and Lowe, *Wealth and Power*, 60-61.

[22] U.S. Census, 1860, Texas [Marion, Harrison, Rusk, Upshur, San Augustine, Anderson, Milam, La Grange, and Robertson Counties]; While researching the recruits of the Nineteenth Texas Infantry, it was necessary to find the listed recruits in their home counties which proved to be an arduous task. While combing through this data, it was possible to compile a spreadsheet that included the age, occupation, family status, and property ownership of thirty-five percent of the men of Company A; Garland E. Robbins, "A History of the Nineteenth Texas Volunteer Infantry, C.S.A." (M.A. Thesis, Lamar University, Beaumont, Tex., 2006), 4-5; Murat Halstead, *A History of the National Political Conventions of the Current Presidential Campaign* (Columbus: Follet, Foster, and Company, 1860), 17.

[23] Lowe, *Walker's Texas Division*, 19-25; United States Department of War, Compiled Service Records of Soldiers Who Served in Organizations from the State of Texas, (Record Group 109, National Archives, Washington, D.C.) Analysis of Company A (hereafter cited as CSR, 19th TX).

[24] Bell I. Wiley, *The Life of Johnny Reb: The Common Soldier of the Confederacy.* (Baton Rouge: Louisiana State University Press, 1943), 22-25.

[25] CSR, 19th TX, Analysis of Company A.

[26] CSR, 19th TX, John B. Snow.

[27] CSR, 19th TX, Charles F. Renean.

[28] CSR, 19th TX, Analysis of Company A.

[29] Ibid.

[30] Wiley, *The Life of Johnny Reb,* 27-29; CSR, 19th TX, Analysis of Company A.

[31] CSR, 19th TX, Analysis of Company A.

[32] Wiley, *The Life of Johnny Reb,* 15-19.

[33] U.S. Census, 1860 [Marion, Rusk, Upshur, San Augustine, Anderson, Milam, La Grange, and Robertson Counties]; Lowe, *Walker's Texas Division*, 19-25; Wiley, *The Life of Johnny Reb,* 25-29.

[34] U.S. Census, 1860 [Marion, Rusk, Upshur, San Augustine, Anderson, Milam, La Grange, and Robertson Counties]; Campbell and Lowe, *Wealth and Power*, 60-61.

[35] U.S. Census, 1860, Texas [Marion, Rusk, Upshur, San Augustine, Anderson, Milam, La Grange, Liberty, and Robertson Counties]; Robbins, "A History of the Nineteenth Texas Volunteer Infantry," 4-5.

[36] CSR, 19th TX, Analysis of Company A.

[37] U.S. Census 1860, TX [Harrison, Marion, and San Augustine Counties].

[38] U.S. Census 1860, TX [Marion and Liberty Counties]; In 2001, *The Journal of Southern History* published Charles E. Brooks' "The Social and Cultural Dynamics of Soldiering in Hood's Texas Brigade." In Brooks' essay, he lays out the economic backgrounds of the men from each of the regiments that formed the brigade. On average, 31 percent of these men were classified as "poor" using the previously qualified standards. This is a substantially higher rate of poor men than those that joined Company A, Nineteenth Texas Infantry.

[39] U.S. Census 1860, TX [Marion, Rusk, Upshur, San Augustine, Anderson, Milam, La Grange, and Robertson Counties]; CSR, 19th TX, W. L. Crawford, G. T. Mott, A. Smith.

[40] Lester N. Fitzhugh, "WALKER'S TEXAS DIVISION," *Handbook of Texas Online* (http://www.tshaonline.org/hand book/online/articles/hgj02), accessed April 1, 2013. Published by the Texas State Historical Association.

[41] Lowe, *Walker's Texas Division,* 41-42.

[42] Ibid., 79-85; Richard Lowe, ed. *Greyhound Commander: Confederate General John G. Walker's History of the Civil War West of the Mississippi* (Baton Rouge: Louisiana State University Press, 2013), 13-14.

[43] U.S. Census, 1860, Texas [Marion, Rusk, Upshur, San Augustine, Anderson, Milam, La Grange, and Robertson Counties].

[44] Christopher Long, "JEFFERSON, TEXAS (MARION COUNTY)," *Handbook of Texas Online* (http://www.tshaonline .org/handbook/online/articles/hgj02), accessed April 1, 2013. Published by the Texas State Historical Association; Fred Tarpley, *Jefferson: Riverport to the Southwest* (Wolfe City, Tex.: Henington Publishing Company, 1983), 60-70.

[45] CSR, 19th TX, Richard Waterhouse.

[46] Thomas W. Cutrer, "WATERHOUSE, RICHARD," *Handbook of Texas Online* (http://www.tshaonline.org/hand book/online/articles/fwa67), accessed April 02, 2013. Published by the Texas State Historical Association.

[47] CSR, 19th TX, Richard Waterhouse; CSR, 19th TX, William Crawford; "Editorial," *The Texas State Gazette* (Austin, Texas), Volume 11, no. 48, July 7, 1860 (accessed from *Geneologybank.com*; http://www.genealogybank.com/gbnk /newspapers/doc/v2:10EEA62CDA4CF8A0@GBNEWS-10F1C907AC2 18410@2400599-10F1C90800907C48@1/?s_ dlid=DL0114050701454509190&s_ecproduct=SUB-Y-6995-R&s_ecprodtype=RENEW-A-R&s_trackval=&s_siteloc=&s_ referrer=&s_subterm=Subscription%20unti l%3A%2001%2 F16%2F2015&s_docsbal=%20&s_subexpires=01%2F16%2F201 5&s_docstart=&s_docsleft=&s_docsread=&s_username=mccasli n@unt.edu&s_accountid=AC0109102002183021847&s_upgrade able=no accessed May 7, 2014).

[48] Blessington, *The Campaigns of Walker's Texas Division*, 19-28.

[49] CSR: 19th TX: M. L. Crawford; Horace Herndon Cunningham, *Doctors in Gray: The Confederate Medical Service* (Baton Rouge: Louisiana State University Press, 1958), 165-166.

[50] CSR; 19th TX, M. L. Crawford; "Confederate Veterans Eulogize M. L. Crawford," *Dallas Morning News* (Dallas, Texas), June 20, 1910.

[51] Ibid.

[52] Lowe, *Walker's Texas Division, C.S.A.*, 226-230; CSR; 19th TX, M. L. Crawford.

[53] Civil War Muster Roll Index Cards (Confederate and Union), Texas State Library and Archives Commission, Austin, Texas; CSR, 19th TX, Jefferson Dale and Marshall N. Dale.

CHAPTER TWO

[54] Joseph P. Blessington, *The Campaigns of Walker's Texas Division: By a Private Soldier* (Austin: Eakin Press, 1968), 29-35.

[55] Ibid., 37.

[56] Richard Lowe, *Walker's Texas Division C.S.A., Greyhounds of the Trans-Mississippi* (Baton Rouge: Louisiana State University Press, 2006), 59-64; H.A. Wallace to My Dear Affectionate Wife, October 26, 1862, Harvey Alexander Wallace Papers, Southwest Arkansas Regional Archives, Washington, Arkansas.

[57] Lowe, *Walker's Texas Division*, 60; Lowe, *Greyhound Commander*, 58-61.

[58] Blessington, *The Campaigns of Walker's Texas Division*, 69-71.

[59] Ralph Wooster, *Texas and Texans in the Civil War* (Austin: Eakin Press, 1995), 74.

[60] Lowe, *Walker's Texas Division,* 59-78.

[61] Lowe, *Walker's Texas Division,* 44-46.

[62] United States Department of War, Compiled Service Records of Soldiers Who Served in Organizations from the State of Texas, (Record Group 109, National Archives, Washington, D.C.) Jefferson Dale and Marshall N. Dale (hereafter cited as CSR, 19th TX); Mark A. Weitz, *More Damning than Slaughter: Desertion in the Confederate Army* (Lincoln: University of Nebraska Press, 2005), 286-287.

[63] Alan Hankinson, *Vicksburg 1863: Grant Clears the Mississippi* (Oxford: Osprey Publishing, 1992), 16.

[64] Lowe, *Walker's Texas Division,* 79-81.

[65] U.S. War Department, *The War of the Rebellion: Official Records of Union and Confederate Armies*, 128 vols. (Washington, D.C.: U. S. Government Printing Office, 1880-1891), Series I, Volume 26, pt. 2, 12-13 (hereafter this source will be cited as *OR* with correct volume and part indicated).

[66] Blessington, *The Campaigns of Walker's Texas Division*, 66-67; Lowe, *Greyhound Commander*, 9-13.

[67] *OR*, Series I, Volume 26, pt. 2, 12-13.

[68] Lowe, *Walker's Texas Division*, 81.

[69] Blessington, *The Campaigns of Walker's Texas Division*, 85.

[70] Ibid., 86-87.

[71] Blessington, *The Campaigns of Walker's Texas Division*, 91; Lowe, *Walker's Texas Division,* 83-85.

[72] Blessington, *The Campaigns of Walker's Texas Division*, 91.

[73] Lowe, *Walker's Texas Division,* 83-85; *OR*, Series I, Volume 23, pt. 1, 464.

[74] *OR*, Series I, Volume 23, pt. 1, 464; Blessington, *The Campaigns of Walker's Texas Division*, 101.

[75] Linda Barnickel, *Millikens Bend: A Civil War Battle in History and Memory* (Baton Rouge: Louisiana State University Press, 2013), 73-81.

[76] *OR,* Series 1, Volume 24, Part 1, 467.

[77] Blessington, *The Campaigns of Walker's Texas Division*, 95-109.

[78] *OR,* Series 1, Volume 24, Part 1,467.

[79] Barnickel, *Milliken's Bend*, 447.

[80] Blessington, *The Campaigns of Walker's Texas Division*, 101-103.

[81] Ibid., 447.

[82] Barnickel, *Milliken's Bend*, 90.

[83] *OR,* Series 1, Volume 24, Part 1, 448.

[84] Blessington, *The Campaigns of Walker's Texas Division*, 98.

[85] Ibid., 96.

[86] *OR,* Series 1, Part 1, Volume 24, 467.

[87] Ibid., 467.

[88] Barnickel, *Milliken's Bend,* 91.

[89] *OR,* Series 1, Part 1, Volume 24, 467.

[90] Blessington, *The Campaigns of Walker's Texas Division,* 98-101.

[91] *OR,* Series 1, Part 2,Volume 24, 453.

[92] Ibid., 464.

[93] Blessington, *The Campaigns of Walker's Texas Division,* 97.

[94] Ibid., 96; *OR,* Series 1, Part 2, Volume 24, 448.

[95] *OR*, Series 1, Volume 24, 467-470.

[96] *OR,* Series 1, Part 1, Volume 24, 447-448; Blessington, *The Campaigns of Walker's Texas Division,* 108.

[97] Barnickel, *Milliken's Bend,* 113-114.

[98] *OR,* Series 1, Part 1, Volume 24, 95-96.

[99] Barnickel, *Milliken's Bend,* 113-114.

[100] Ibid.

[101] Lowe, *Walker's Texas Division,* 97-101.

[102] George S. Burkhardt, *Confederate Rage, Yankee Wrath: No Quarter in the Civil War* (Carbondale: Southern Illinois University Press, 2007), 58-68; Lowe, *Walker's Texas Division,* 96-101; *OR,* Series 1, Part 1, Volume 24, 95-96.

[103] Burkhardt, *Confederate Rage, Yankee Wrath,* 58-68; Lowe, *Walker's Texas Division,* 96-101; *OR,* Series 1, Part 1, Volume 24, 95-96.

[104] *OR,* Series 2, Volume 6, 115.

[105] *OR,* Series 1, Volume 24, 467-470.

[106] Ibid., 447-448.

[107] CSR, 19th TX, A. Bradshaw, C. C. Malone, R. N. Neal, William Rollins; Garland Robbins, "A History of the Nineteenth Texas Volunteer Infantry, C. S. A." (M.A. Thesis., Lamar University, Beaumont, Tex., 2006), 65.

[108] James M. McPherson, *Battle Cry of Freedom: The Civil War Era* (New York: Oxford University Press, 1988), 476; Blessington, *The Campaigns of Walker's Texas Division,* 95-109; CSR, 19th TX, A. Bradshaw.

[109] Ibid.

[110] Lowe, *Walker's Texas Division,* 148-165.

[111] "The Fight at Millken's Bend," *Harper's Weekly,* July 4, 1863.

[112] Blessington, *The Campaigns of Walker's Texas Division,* 182-200.

[113] Barnickel, *Milliken's Bend,* 165.

[114] Ibid., 174-175.

[115] Barnickel, *Milliken's Bend*, 48-81; Blessington, *The Campaigns of Walker's Texas Division*, 76-77; Lowe, *Walker's Texas Division*, 78.

[116] *OR,* Series 1, Part 1, Volume 24, 470.

CHAPTER THREE

[117] Richard Lowe, *Walker's Texas Division, C.S.A.: Greyhounds of the Trans-Mississippi* (Baton Rouge: Louisiana State University Press, 2004), 169; Stephen A. Dupree, *Planting the Union Flag in Texas: The Campaigns of Major General Nathaniel P. Banks in the West* (College Station: Texas A&M University Press, 2008), 108-140; Joe Walker, *Harvest of Death: The Battle of Jenkins' Ferry, Arkansas* (Private Publishing, 2012), 30-37, 130-147.

[118] Colonel Richard Waterhouse, Jr. to Rose Waterhouse, February 15, 1863, Richard, Waterhouse, Jr., Letters, 1858-1872, University of Arkansas at Little Rock Institute for History and Culture, Little Rock, Arkansas.

[119] Joseph P. Blessington, *The Campaigns of Walker's Texas Division: By a Private Soldier* (Austin: The Pemberton Press, 1968), 66-71.

[120] Ibid., 95-102; U.S. War Department, *The War of the Rebellion: Official Records of Union and Confederate Armies*, 128 vols. (Washington, D.C.: U. S. Government Printing Office, 1880-1891), Series I, Volume 23, pt. 1, 467 (hereafter this source will be cited as *OR*).

[121] Lowe, *Walker's Texas Division*, 104-115, 134-135.

[122] Lowe, *Walker's Texas Division*, 104-115, 134-135, United States Department of War, Compiled Service Records of Soldiers Who Served in Organizations from the State of Texas, (Record Group 109, National Archives, Washington, D.C.), W. J. Clark and William L. Crawford (hereafter cited as CSR, 19th TX); Thomas W. Cutrer, "SCURRY, WILLIAM READ, " *Handbook of Texas Online* (http://www.tshaonline.org/ handbook /online/ articles/fsc38), accessed May 17, 2014. Uploaded on June 15, 2010. Modified on March 8, 2011. Published by the Texas State Historical Association.

[123] Blessington, *The Campaigns of Walker's Texas Division*, 150-154.

[124] CSR, 19th TX, Analysis of Company A; Garland Robbins, "A History of the Nineteenth Texas Volunteer Infantry, C. S. A." (M.A. Thesis., Lamar University, Beaumont, Tex., 2006), 187-196.

[125] Richard Taylor, *Destruction and Reconstruction: Personal Experiences of the Late War* (London: William Blackwood and Sons, 1879), 113-115.

[126] Ralph Wooster, *Texas and Texans in the Civil War* (Austin: Eakin Press, 1995), 139.

[127] *OR,* Series I, Vol. 34, 314.

[128] Blessington, *The Campaigns of Walker's Texas Division*, 174.

[129] Reid Mitchell, *Civil War Soldiers* (New York: Simon & Schuster, 1988), 78.

[130] Lowe, *Walker's Texas Division,* 117.

[131] Blessington, *The Campaigns of Walker's Texas Division*, 179.

[132] Lowe, *Walker's Texas Division,* 189.

[133] Blessington, *The Campaigns of Walker's Texas Division,* 193.

[134] Lowe, *Walker's Texas Division,* 190-192.

[135] *OR,* Series I, Volume 23, pt. 1, 341; Blessington, *The Campaigns of Walker's Texas Division,* 193-200; Lowe, *Walker's Texas Division,* 206.

[136] Alwyn Barr, "Texan Losses in the Red River Campaign," *Military History of Texas* 3 (Summer 1963), 103-110; *OR,* Series I, Vol. 34, 341-346; Henry C. Joiner, "The Youngest Son of a Veteran,"*Confederate Veteran,* November 1905, 496; *OR,* Series I, Volume 23, pt. 1, 341.

[137] *OR,* Series I, Vol. 34, 568.

[138] *OR,* Series I, Vol. 34, 568; Lowe, *Walker's Texas Division,* 212.

[139] Lowe, *Walker's Texas Division,* 213.

[140] Blessington, *The Campaigns of Walker's Texas Division,* 243; Lowe, *Walker's Texas Division,* 214-217.

[141] Blessington, *The Campaigns of Walker's Texas Division,* 248; Lowe, *Walker's Texas Division,* 222.

[142] Blessington, *The Campaigns of Walker's Texas Division,* 253-256; *Walker's Texas Division,* 225-226.

[143] Robbins, "A History of the Nineteenth Texas Volunteer Infantry," 146; Barr, "Texan Losses in the Red River Campaign, 1864," 106-107.

[144] Lowe, *Walker's Texas Division,* 230.

102

[145] Blessington, *The Campaigns of Walker's Texas Division*, 261.

[146] Ibid., 263.

[147] Ibid; "To the Citizens of Texas," *Houston Daily Telegraph* (Houston, Texas), August 12, 1864 (accessed from Geneologybank.com, http://www.genealogybank.com/gbnk /newspapers/ doc/v2:10EEA6D834E2E508@GBNEWS-10F1E5971269E1E8@2402096-10F1E597298B8750@0 /?&s_dlid=DL0114042918180902093&s_ecproduct=SUB-Y-6995-R&s_ecprodtype=RENEW-A-R&s_track val=&s_ siteloc=&s_referrer=&s_subterm=Subscription %20until %3A%2001%2F16%2F2015&s_docsbal=% 20&s_subexpires= 01%2F16%2F2015&s_docstart=&s_docsleft=&s_docsread=&s_u sername=mccaslin@unt.edu&s_accountid=AC01091020021830 21847&s_upgradeable=no&s_dlid=DL0114042918181502121&s _ecproduct=SUB-Y-6995-R&s_ecprodtype=RENEW-A-R&s_trackval=&s_siteloc=&s_referrer=&s_subterm=Subscripti on %20until%3A%2001%2F16%2F2015&s_docsbal=%20&s_ subexpires=01%2F16%2F2015&s_docstart=&s_docsleft=&s_doc sread=&s_username=mccaslin@unt.edu&s_accountid=AC01091 02002183021847&s_upgradeable=no, accessed April 29, 2014).

[148] Lowe, *Walker's Texas Division,* 235.

[149] Ibid., 240.

[150] Blessington, *The Campaigns of Walker's Texas Division*, 277.

[151] Lowe, *Walker's Texas Division*, 245.

[152] Blessington, *The Campaigns of Walker's Texas Division*, 298.

[153] Lowe, *Walker's Texas Division*, 250.

[154] Lowe, *Walker's Texas Division*, 255; Captain B.B. Paddock, ed., *A Twentieth Century History and Biographical Record of North and West Texas* (Chicago: Lewis Publishing Company, 1906), 126-128; "Camp Near Hempstead," *Houston Tri-weekly Telegraph*, May 17, 1865, Volume 31, Issue 23 (accessed fromGeneology bank.com, http://www.genealogybank.com/gbnk/newspapers/doc/v2:1428926F 567957 C9@GB NEWS -10F1C1F2F041A 728@2402374-10F1C1 F32DB25D40@1/?& sdlid =DL0114042917363328320&s_ecproduct= SUB -Y-6995-R&s_ecprodtype=RENEW-A-R&s_trackval=&s_siteloc= &s_ referrer=&s_subterm=Subscription %20until%3A%2001%2F16 %2F2015&s_docsbal=%20&s_subexpires=01%2F16%2F2015&s _docstart=&s_docsleft=&s_docsread=&s_username=mccaslin@ unt.edu&s_accountid=AC0109102002183021847&s_upgradeabl e=no, accessed April 30, 2014).

[155] Ibid.

[156] Ibid., 214.

CHAPTER FOUR

[157] Richard Lowe, *Walker's Texas Division, C.S.A.: Greyhounds of the Trans-Mississippi* (Baton Rouge: Louisiana State University Press, 2006), 250-255.

[158] Civil War Muster Rolls Index Cards (both Confederate and Union), Texas State Library and Archives Commission, Austin, Texas; United States Department of War, Compiled Service Records of Soldiers Who Served in Organizations from the State of Texas, (Record Group 109, National Archives, Washington, D.C.), analysis of Company A (hereafter cited as CSR , 19th TX,); Garland Robbins, "A History of the Nineteenth Texas Volunteer Infantry, C. S. A." (M.A. Thesis., Lamar University, Beaumont, Tex., 2006), 4-5.

[159] United States Department of the Interior, Bureau of the Census, Eighth Census, 1860, Texas [Marion, Rusk, Upshur, San Augustine, Anderson, Milam, La Grange, and Robertson Counties] Record Group 29, National Archives, Washington, D.C.; (hereafter cited as U.S. Census with appropriate decade and county designation); U.S. Census, 1860, Louisiana [Orleans Parish]; U.S. Census, 1860, Mississippi [Harrison County].

[160] "Richard Waterhouse and Son," *The Eastern Texian* (San Augustine, Texas), Volume 1, no. 37, December 12, 1857 (accessed from *The Portal to Texas History* courtesy of the University of North Texas; http://texashistory.unt.edu/ark: /67531/metapth233687/m1/4/, accessed October 10, 2013); Thomas W. Cutrer, "WATERHOUSE, RICHARD," *Handbook of Texas Online* (http://www.tshaonline.org/handbook/ online /articles/hgj02), accessed February 2, 2014. Published by the Texas State Historical Association.

[161] Colonel Richard Waterhouse, Jr. to Richard S. Waterhouse, February 18, 1863, Richard Waterhouse, Jr., Letters, 1858-1872, University of Arkansas at Little Rock Institute for History and Culture, Little Rock, Arkansas; Thomas W. Cutrer, "WATERHOUSE, RICHARD," *Handbook of Texas Online* (http://www.tshaonline. org/handbook/online /articles/hgj02), accessed February 2, 2014. Published by the Texas State Historical Association.

162 Colonel Richard Waterhouse, Jr. to W.H. Wallace, January 2, 1866, Richard Waterhouse, Jr., Letters, 1858-1872, University of Arkansas at Little Rock Institute for History and Culture, Little Rock, Arkansas.; "Names of persons pardoned by the President," House Executive Document 116, March 2, 1867, Serial Set Number 1293, 74 (accessed at Geneologybank .com, http://www.genealogybank.com/gbnk/documents/doc /v2:0FD2A62D41CEB699@GBDOC-1097B63493450F48@/? search_terms=waterhouse%7Crichard &s_dlid=DL011404291 8342404435&s_ecproduct=SUB-Y-6995-R&s_ecprodtype=RE NEW-A-R&s_trackval=&s_siteloc=&s_ referrer=&s_subterm =Subscription%20until%3A%2001%2F16%2F2015&s_docsbal= %20&s_subexpires=01%2F16%2F2015&s_docstart=&s_docsleft =&s_docsread=&s_username=mccaslin@unt.edu&s_accountid= AC0109102002183021847&s_upgradeable=no, accessed April 30, 2014).

163 Fred Tarpley, *Jefferson: Riverport to the Southwest* (Wolf City, Tex.: Henington Publishing Company, 1983), 96-97.

164 U.S. Census, 1870, Texas [San Augustine County].

165 Cutrer, "WATERHOUSE," *Handbook of Texas Online.*

166 Weldon Nash and Mitchell Whitington, *Civil War Veterans of Jefferson's Oakwood Cemetery* (Jefferson, Tex.: Private Printing in Cooperation with Jefferson Historical Society and Museum, 2012), 34.

167 CSR, 19th TX, M.W. Covey; Texas Marriage Collection, Marriage Record of Maranda Covey and Susan Gannt, *Ancestry.com*, last modified February 2014, accessed February 5, 2014.

[168]Jaques D. Bagur, *Antebellum Jefferson, Texas: Everyday Life in an East Texas Town* (Denton, University of North Texas Press, 2012), 499; U.S. Census, 1860, Texas [Marion County]; "Searching for Missing Friends," *Boston Pilot*, 26 August 1865; "R.B. Smithson," *Findagrave*, last updated February 2014, accessed February 10, http://www.findagrave.com /cgi-bin/fg.cgi?page=gr&GSln=SMIT&GSfn=R&G Spart ial=1&G Sbyrel=all&GSst=46&GScntry=4&GSsr=4001&GRid= 8100982&.

[169] U.S. Census, 1860, Texas [Marion County]; U.S. Census, 1870, Texas [Marion County]; U.S. Census, 1880, Texas [Marion County]; "R. B. Smithson," Findagrave.com, last updated February 2014, accessed May 13, 2014, http://www findagrave.com/cgi-bin/fg.cgi?page=gr&GSln=Smithson &GSbyrel=all&GSdy= 1890&GSdyrel=before&GSst=46 &GScntry =4&GSob=n&GRid=8100982&df=all&.

[170] U.S. Census, 1870, Texas [Dallas County]; U.S. Census, 1880, Texas [Dallas County]; U.S. Census, 1900, Texas [Dallas County]; "William Jefferson Clark," Findagrave.com, last modified February 2014, accessed February 10, 2014, http://www.findagrave.com/cgi-bin/fg.cgi?page=gr&GSln =CLARK&GSfn=WILLIAM &GSmn=JEFFERSON&GSbyrel =all&GSdy=1920&GSdyrel=before&GSst=46&GScntry=4&GSo b=n&GRid=24566872&df=all&.

[171] U.S. Census, Texas, 1870 [Galveston County]; U.S. Census, 1880, Texas [Dallas County]; U.S. Census, 1900, Texas [Dallas County].

[172] John W. Leonard, ed., *Who's Who in America: A Biographical Dictionary of Notable Living Men and Women of the United States* (Chicago: A. N. Marquis & Company Publishers, 1901), 254; "William Lynne Crawford," Texas State Legislative Reference Library, last modified August 5, 2013, accessed February 3, 2014, http://www.lrl.state.tx.us/mobile /memberDisplay.cfm?memberID=3731.

[173] Robert W. Stayton, ed., *Proceeding of the Annual State Bar of Texas* (Dallas: Wilkinson Printing Company, 1922), 194.

[174] "William Lynne Crawford," Texas State Legislative Reference Library, last modified August 5, 2013, accessed February 3, 2014, http://www.lrl.state.tx.us/mobile /member Display.cfm?memberID=3731; Thomas W. Cutrer, "CRAW FORD, WILLIAM LYNNE," *Handbook of Texas Online* (http://www.tshaonline.org/handbook/ online/articles/hgj02), accessed February 4, 2014. Published by the Texas State Historical Association.

[175] Captain B.B. Paddock, ed., *A Twentieth Century History and Biographical Record of North and West Texas* (Chicago: Lewis Publishing Company, 1906), 126-128.

[176] Ibid.; Stephanie P. Niemeyer, "TAYLOR, ENNIS WARD," *Handbook of Texas Online* (http://www.tshaonline. org/handbook/online/articles/hgj02), accessed February 6, 2014. Published by the Texas State Historical Association; CSR, 19th TX, E.W. Taylor, U.S. Census, 1860, Texas [Marion County]; U.S. Census, 1870, Texas [Marion County].

[177] Paddock, *A History of North and West Texas*, 126-129; Niemeyer, "ENNIS WARD TAYLOR," *Handbook of Texas Online*; Col. Gary W. Canada, *History of the 19th Texas Infantry Confederate States Army*, ed. Edward R. DeVries (Privately Published, 2006), 61.

[178] Ibid.; "Ennis Ward Taylor" *Findagrave*, last updated February 2014, accessed February 10, 2014, http://www.find agrave.com/cgi-bin/fg.cgi?page=gr&GSln=taylor&GSfn=ennis &GSmn=ward&GSbyrel =all&GSdyrel=all&GSst=46&GScntry =4&GSob=n&GRid=8891718&df=all&.

[179] CSR, 19th TX, Aaron C. Smith.

[180] U.S. Census, 1860, Texas [Marion, Rusk, Upshur, San Augustine, Anderson, Milam, La Grange, and Robertson Counties]; Death Certificate for Aaron C. Smith, 2 August, 1925, File Number 23339, Texas State Board of Health, Bureau of Vital Statistics (accessed at Ancestry.com February 5, 2014).

[181] U.S. Census, 1860, Texas [Marion County]; U.S. Census, 1870, Texas [Marion County]; CSR, 19th TX, Henry McLaughlin.

[182] CSR, 19th TX, A.K. Northrop.

[183] U.S. Census, 1860, Texas [San Augustine County]; U.S. Census, 1880, Mississippi [Harrison County].

[184] Civil War Muster Rolls Index Cards (both Confederate and Union). Texas State Library and Archives Commission, Austin, Texas.

[185] CSR, 19th TX, J. Dale and M.N. Dale.

[186] Lowe, *Walker's Texas Division, C.S.A.,* 44-46; U.S. Census, 1870, Texas [Washington County]; CSR, 19th TX, J. Dale.

[187] U.S. Census, 1860, Texas [Marion County]; U.S. Census, 1870, Texas [Marion County]; CSR, F. Morgan.

[188] U.S. Census, 1860, Texas [Marion, Rusk, Upshur, San Augustine, Anderson, Milam, La Grange, and Robertson Counties]; U.S. Census, 1870, Texas [Marion, Rusk, Upshur, San Augustine, Anderson, Milam, La Grange, and Robertson Counties]; U.S. Census, 1880, Texas [Marion, Rusk, Upshur, San Augustine, Anderson, Milam, La Grange, and Robertson Counties].

BIBLIOGRAPHY

Primary Sources
Unpublished
Civil War Muster Rolls Index Cards (both Confederate and Union). Texas State Library and Archives Commission, Austin, Texas.

Texas State Board of Health, Bureau of Vital Statistics. Austin, Texas.

Texas State Library and Archives Commission. Civil War Muster Roll Index Cards (both Union and Confederate. Austin, Texas.

United States. Department of the Interior. Bureau of the Census. Eighth Census, 1860. Record Group 29. National Archives, Washington, D.C.

United States. Department of the Interior. Bureau of the Census. Ninth Census, 1870. Record Group 29. National Archives, Washington, D.C.

United States. Department of the Interior. Bureau of the Census. Tenth Census, 1880. Record Group 29. National Archives, Washington, D.C.

United States. Department of the Interior. Bureau of the Census. Twelfth Census, 1900. Record Group 29. National Archives, Washington, D.C.

United States, Department of War. Compiled Service Records of Confederate Soldiers Who Served in Organizations from Texas. Record Group 109, National Archives, Washington, D.C.

Wallace, Harvey Alexander Papers. Southwest Arkansas Regional Archives. Washington, Arkansas.

Waterhouse, Richard Jr. Papers, 1858-1872. University of Arkansas at Little Rock. Institute for History and Culture. Little Rock, Arkansas.

Published

Blessington, J.P. *The Campaigns of Walker's Texas Division: By a Private Soldier*. Austin: The Pemberton Press, 1968.

Joiner, Henry. "The Youngest Son of a Veteran." *Confederate Veteran,* November 1905, 496-497.

Halstead, Murat. *A History of the National Political Conventions of the Current Presidential Campaign*. Columbus: Follet, Foster, and Company, 1860.

Lowe, Richard, ed. *Greyhound Commander: Confederate General John G. Walker's History of the Civil War West of the Mississippi.* Baton Rouge: University of Louisiana Press, 2013.

Taylor, Richard. *Destruction and Reconstruction: Personal Experiences of the Late War.* London: William Blackwood and Sons, 1879.

United States Department of War. *The War of the Rebellion: A Compilation of the Official Records of the Union and Confederate Armies,* 128 vols. Washington, D. C.: Government Printing Office, 1880-1902.

United States. House of Representatives. "Names of Persons Pardoned by the President." House Executive Document Number 116. Thirty-ninth Congress, Second Session, Serial Set Volume 1293.

Newspapers

Boston Pilot. Boston, Mass. 1865.

Dallas Morning News. Dallas, Tex. 1910.

Eastern Texian. San Augustine, Tex. 1857.

Harper's Weekly. New York, New York. 1863.

Houston Daily Telegraph. Houston, Tex. 1862-1865.

Houston Triweekly Telegraph. Houston, Tex. 1862-1865.

The Texas State Gazette. Austin, Tex. 1860.

Secondary Sources
Articles
Angle, Paul M. "Lincoln's Power with Words." *Papers of the Abraham Lincoln Association* 3 (1981): 8-27.

Barr, Alwyn. "Texan Losses in the Red River Campaign." *Military History of Texas* 3 (Summer 1963): 103-110.

Brooks, Charles E. "The Social and Cultural Dynamics of Soldiering in Hood's Texas Brigade." *The Journal of Southern History* 67 (August 2001): 535-572.

Johnson, Ludwell H. "Fort Sumter and Confederate Diplomacy." *The Journal of Southern History* 26 (November 1960): 441-477.

Mahon, John K. "Civil War Infantry Assault Tactics." *Military Affairs* 25 (Summer 1961): 57-68.

Books
Bagur, Jaques D. *Antebellum Jefferson, Texas: Everyday Life in an East Texas Town*. Denton, Texas: University of North Texas Press, 2012.

Barnickel, Linda. *Millikens Bend: A Civil War Battle in History and Memory*. Baton Rouge: Louisiana State University Press, 2013.

Burkhardt, George S. *Confederate Rage, Yankee Wrath: No Quarter in the Civil War.* Carbondale: Southern Illinois University Press, 2007.

Campbell, Randolph B. *Gone to Texas: A History of the Lone Star State*. Oxford: Oxford University Press, 2003.

Campbell, Randolph B., and Richard G. Lowe. *Wealth and Power in Antebellum Texas*. College Station: Texas A & M University Press, 1977.

Canada, Col. Gary W. *History of the 19th Texas Infantry Confederate States Army*. Edited by Edward R. DeVries. Private Publishing, 2006.

Cunningham, Horace Herndon. *Doctors in Gray: The Confederate Medical Service*. Baton Rouge: Louisiana State University Press, 1958.

Cutrer, Thomas W. *Ben McCulloch and the Frontier Military Tradition*. Chapel Hill: University of North Carolina Press, 1993.

Dupree, Stephen A. *Planting the Union Flag in Texas: The Campaigns of Major General Nathanial P. Banks in the West.* College Station: Texas A&M University Press, 2008.

Hankinson, Alan. *Vicksburg 1863: Grant Clears the Mississippi.* Oxford: Osprey Publishing, 1992.

Leonard, John W. ed., *Who's Who in America: A Biographical Dictionary of Notable Living Men and Women of the United States.* Chicago: A.N. Marquis & Company Publishers, 1901.

Lowe, Richard G. *Walker's Texas Division, C.S.A., The Greyhounds of the Trans-Mississippi.* Baton Rouge: Louisiana State University Press, 2006.

McCaslin, Richard B. *Fighting Stock: John S. "Rip" Ford of Texas.* Fort Worth: Texas Christian University Press, 2011.

McPherson, James M. *Battle Cry of Freedom: The Civil War Era.* Oxford: Oxford University Press, 1988.

Millett, Allen R., and Peter Maslowski. *For the Common Defense: A Military History of the United States of America.* New York: Free Press, 1994.

Mitchell, Reid. *Civil War Soldiers*. New York: Simon & Schuster, 1988.

Moore, Albert Burton. *Conscription and Conflict in the Confederacy*. Columbia: University of South Carolina Press, 1924.

Nash, Weldon and Mitchell Whitington, *Civil War Veterans of Jefferson's Oakwood Cemetery*. Jefferson, Tex.: Private Printing in Cooperation with Jefferson Historical Society and Museum, 2012.

Paddock, Captain B.B., ed., *A Twentieth Century History and Biographical Record of North and West Texas*. Chicago: Lewis Publishing Company, 1906.

Stayton, Robert W., ed., *Proceedings of the Annual State Bar of Texas*. Dallas: Wilkinson Printing Company, 1922.

Tarpley, Fred. *Jefferson: Riverport to the Southwest*. Wolfe City, Tex.: Henington Publishing Company, 1983.

Walker, Joe. *Harvest of Death: The Battle of Jenkins' Ferry, Arkansas*. Privately published, 2012.

Weigley, Russell F. *The American Way of War*. Bloomington: Indiana University Press, 1967.

Weitz, Mark A. *More Damning than Slaughter: Desertion in the Confederate Army*. Lincoln: University of Nebraska Press, 2005.

Wiley, Bell I. *The Life of Johnny Reb: The Common Soldier of the Confederacy*. Baton Rouge: Louisiana State University Press, 1943.

Wooster, Ralph. *Texas and Texans in the Civil War*. Austin: Eakin Press, 1995.

Online Resources

Cutrer, Thomas W. "SCURRY, WILLIAM READ," *Handbook of Texas Online* (http://www.tsha online.org/handbook/online/articles/hgj02), accessed April 2, 2013. Published by the Texas State Historical Association.

Cutrer, Thomas W. "WATERHOUSE, RICHARD," *Handbook of Texas Online* (http://www.tsha online.org/handbook/online/articles/fwa67), accessed April 02, 2013. Published by the Texas State Historical Association.

Fitzhugh, Lester N. "WALKER'S TEXAS DIVISION," *Handbook of Texas Online* (http://www.tshaonline.org/handbook/online/ar ticles/hgj02), accessed April 1, 2013. Published by the Texas State Historical Association.

Long, Christopher. "JEFFERSON, TEXAS (MARION COUNTY)," *Handbook of Texas Online* (http://www.tshaonline.org/hand book/online/articles/hgj02), accessed April 1, 2013. Published by the Texas State Historical Association.

Park, David. "19th TEXAS INFANTRY," *Handbook of Texas Online* (http://www.tshaonline.org/ handbook/online/articles/hgj02), accessed April 5, 2013. Published by the Texas State Historical Association.

"Abraham Lincoln Papers," Library of Congress, Last Updated 2013, accessed October 21, 2013, http://memory.loc.gov/cgi-bin/query /P?mal:8:./temp/~ammem_8VyO.

Thesis/Dissertations

Robbins, Garland E., "A History of the Nineteenth Texas Volunteer Infantry, C.S.A." M.A. Thesis, Lamar University, Beaumont, TX, 2006.

INDEX

About the Author

David Williams lives in Fort Worth, Texas with his wife Amanda and his three children, Nathan, Carter, and Brooklyn. David received his bachelor's degree from the University of Texas at Arlington and his master's degree from the University of North Texas. His study concentrated on American history with an emphasis on the American Civil War resulting in this work on the Nineteenth Texas Infantry, Company A. Additionally, David has authored several articles on topics ranging from local history to unit history that have been published in a variety of historical journals. Currently, David teaches U.S. history at both North Side High School and Tarrant County College. David enjoys Civil War reenacting, traveling, bicycling, and any activity that brings him closer to his family.

www.ingramcontent.com/pod-product-compliance
Lightning Source LLC
Chambersburg PA
CBHW070452090426
42735CB00012B/2517